Cycling
Instructo
Manual

Cycling Instructor's Manual

Version 8.0

©Cycle Training UK Limited
Written by David Dansky
(Based on the original manual
written by Simeon Bamford
and Vicky Carnegy)

Unit 215
Building J
100 Clements Road
London SE16 4DG

020 7231 6005
info@cycletraining.co.uk
www.cycletraining.co.uk

About Cycle Training UK

CTUK is a not-for-profit workers' co operative (registered in England and Wales number 4369994). The business was founded by Sim Bamford in 1998 and registered as a company in 2002. We were then one of only a handful of people providing cycle training and became one of the key players in the cycling revolution of the past decade.

Back then we existed to promote cycling as a sustainable form of transport. We still do. We deliver training that meets and exceeds the UK's National Standards, standards we helped to develop. We believe that the best way to promote cycling is to teach people to use their bikes skillfully and so develop the confidence to ride.

Our values include cycling promotion, training for everyone and training in realistic conditions. We think that cycling is a simple and sustainable activity. We teach people to cooperate with other road users and, of course, to have fun on their bicycles!

We have trained over 70,000 people to cycle confidently and over 1,300 instructors to train people to cycle confidently!

Thanks

Many thanks to Sim Bamford and Vicky Carnegy for their book Cycle Training Instructor's Manual on which this is based. Thanks also to Jean Mowbray for editing and proofreading. Also to Rob James, Eric Chasseray and James Kelly for additional proofreading. Many of the pictures were provided by Will Melling. A special thank you to our wonderful designer Jonathan Spearman-Oxx and to all the instructors of CTUK past and present without whom this book would not have been written.

David Dansky
Head of Training and Development

Contents

1.
The National Standard and Bikeability

In this chapter we will explore the background and development of the National Standard (NS) for cycle training including its aims and history. We will explain how Bikeability fits in with the NS and list the detailed outcomes achieved by trainee cyclists as they go through the syllabus.

'The one-to-one training was really instrumental in overcoming my fear of falling off my bike. I can't emphasise that enough. I now cycle in a highly confident yet safe, low risk way in heavy traffic'

Trainee Bernadette after training – from being a wobbly cyclist she is now commuting 13 miles each way.

1.1 Why teach people to ride bikes?

Someone taught to ride will do so more efficiently, with less risk, enjoy riding and be more likely to choose a bicycle as their mode of transport. By the time they reach the end of a course a person will know how to check their bike, they will be able to control their bike well, will have learnt how to interact with other road users and ridden in a variety of environments including busy roads. They will be happy to ride anywhere where cycling is allowed. Getting more people making more trips by bike, and doing so with minimum risk, is beneficial to themselves and to society. Cycling makes people healthier and the spaces where we live more pleasant.

1.2 Who needs cycle training?

Anyone who already uses a bike or who would like to cycle would benefit from training. As with any skill, input from an expert will improve the way a person does something. Within a couple of hours of training an adult who lacks confidence to use the roads will be able to begin to ride to work. Following a schools course a young person will have the skills to cycle to school if their parents also get training they will more likely allow their child to ride because they will appreciate that cycling isn't very risky). Even an experienced rider will learn new techniques and will ride through traffic more efficiently. As you train to become an instructor you may well find your riding style changes significantly. It is worth focusing on this process since it will help you understand how, as an instructor, you are able to help someone else hone their skills.

Worried about a lost generation of cyclists in the UK, the CTC and The Road Safety Officers Association (LARSOA) brought together an expert group (Called the Cycle Training Reference Group -CTRG) to agree a syllabus and delivery methodology. Members of this group included Cycle Training UK, Life Cycle, Bikeright and the City of York Council; RoSPA, British and Scottish Cycling,The Department for Transport, Transport for London and others.

1.3 What is the National Standard for cycle training?

The National Standard (NS) is a syllabus, a set of riding outcomes, which describes the skills required to become an expert cyclist. This guidance was developed through a consultation process by a group of interested parties in order to ensure that people across the country are being taught the same material. Prior to this, cycling proficiency was being delivered largely in school playgrounds and very quiet roads by people who did not necessarily cycle. The quality of this delivery varied across the UK.

The National Standard guidelines for adults and teenagers were launched in May 2003 followed by guidance for training children in 2004. During this period the Department for Transport funded the training of 100 instructors by four Instructor Training Providers. The number of Instructor Training Providers, now called Instructor Training Organisations (ITOs), grew and most Local Authorities have adopted the Standard.

In 2012 there was a revision of the NS which clarified some anomalies and brought the adult and child standard together in one comprehensive document. Many organisations contributed to this revision including the ITOs and the recently launched body representing the sector, The Association of Bikeability Schemes (TABS). The British Government has backed the scheme throughout and continues to fund the training. The Department for Transport has worked with TABS to set up a quality assurance system recognising the importance of high quality professional training as crucial to getting more people cycling.

National Standard training is divided into three levels:

Level 1 takes place in traffic free spaces. On completion of this level the rider will have excellent bike control, will understand basic bike mechanics and will know how what they wear affects their cycling. They will be able to share these spaces with walkers and other riders.

Level 2 is on road. By the end of this level a person will be able to share the road by understanding how to get seen, communicate and cooperate with other road users. They will have an understanding of The Highway Code and be able to use a variety of infrastructure.

Level 3 takes place on more complex busy A-roads. At the end of Level 3 a trainee will have learnt advanced road positioning and have developed a strong and assertive riding style. They will be able to flow with the traffic, have excellent awareness of potential hazards and be able to manage risk. They will be confident to ride anywhere.

NS training takes place in realistic conditions, using real roads. Trainee cyclists are not tested but observed performing manoeuvres and communicating with drivers. They are assessed on an ongoing basis and move through the syllabus at their own pace. The training is progressive meaning that trainees should be learning at the edge of their comfort zone (where people learn best). They should be continually challenged. As an instructor you will enjoy the fact that many people upskill fairly rapidly.

In addition to these trainee outcomes there are a set of outcomes for National Standard Instructors (NSIs) which are described in the next chapter. You will be observed demonstrating these over the 4 days of the instructor training course and during your Post Course Assessment. There is also an assistant instructor qualification (NSAI), delivered over a 2 day course. Experienced instructors who work for an ITO can become instructor trainers (NSITs) through a further 2 days of training.

1.4 **What is Bikeability?**

Bikeability is a public friendly brand name for the NS training. Organisations that want to deliver NS cycle training register their scheme with the Department for Transport. Their application is successful if they meet the requirements to deliver NS cycle training Once an organisation has been registered as a Bikeability scheme they are allowed to use a set of materials and branding including certificates and badges which make NS cycle training very attractive to young people (and many adults).

On completion of each level badges are awarded. A red badge for completion of Level 1, orange for Level 2 and green (good to go!) for Level 3. Schemes that have registered can join the trade body The Association of Bikeability Schemes (TABS). Registered schemes also fall under the quality assurance system and will need to renew their registration on a regular basis which ensures that delivery of NS training is to the highest quality.

In addition to the many local authority (LA) Bikeability Schemes there are other Bikeability schemes including School Sports Partnerships, private companies, charities, not for profit businesses and cooperatives (like CTUK). These LA Bikeability schemes are able to (part-) fund training through a government grant. Some LAs deliver in-house training and some use the funds to commission training using a Bikeability registered provider.

Since Bikeability was launched, the name, branding and materials have become better known. You will find that often the term Bikeability and National Standard are used interchangeably. The strapline that Bikeability is 'Cycling proficiency for the 21st century' acted as a bridge to explain the term initially and has largely been dropped as the Bikeability brand has become more widely

recognised. It is worth remembering, however, that you are only able to describe NS training as Bikeability and yourself as a Bikeability instructor if you work for a Bikeability registered scheme.

Over the past ten years the sector has grown, become professional and mature. Over the same period there has been a resurgence of cycling in many towns and cities across the UK. As more and more people are undergoing training and taking to riding on bikes, some of the spaces where we live and work are becoming transformed. Many professional drivers are now getting cycle training in order to learn how to share space with people on bikes. A new generation of people are discovering that riding a bicycle is great fun!

1.5 The 3 levels

The table on the next page lists the headings of the 3 levels of trainee outcomes. The numbering and some wording varies slightly from the officially published materials (http://www.dft.gov.uk/bikeability/the-three-levels/). This because it is often possible to join some riding outcomes together to make teaching easier and the riding activity more coherent. It is also handy to have the whole syllabus on one piece of paper. If you work for a Bikeability scheme you may notice slight variations in the order and numbering of these outcomes. The actual riding you teach/observe should not deviate from that described in the official published documentation.

2.0 National Standard Trainee Outcomes

Level ①

1.1	Demonstrate an understanding of safety equipment and clothing and how clothing could make you more visible
1.2	Carry out a simple bike check including checking air, brakes, chain and direction of steering (ABCD)
1.3	Get on and off the bike
1.4	Start off and pedal
1.5	Stop the bike
1.6	Ride along independently (for at least a minute)
1.7	Make the bike go where you want
1.8	Use gears (where the bike has gears)
1.9	Stop quickly with control
1.10	Swerve to avoid objects
1.11	Look all around including behind
1.12	Signal right and left
1.13	*Share space with pedestrians and other cyclists*

Outcomes in italics are optional

You can control your bike in traffic free spaces and are ready to ride on road

Level 2

2.0	Level 1 outcomes
2.1	Start an on-road journey
2.2	Finish an on-road journey
2.3	Be aware of everything around, including behind
2.4	Understand how and when to signal intentions to other road users
2.5	Understand where to ride on roads being used including when to ride in primary and when in secondary position
2.6	Pass parked cars and slower moving vehicles to their right
2.7	Pass side roads *and crossroads riding along the major road*
2.8	Turn right into a major road, do a u-turn then left into a minor road
2.9	Turn left into a major road and right into a minor road
2.10	Explain decisions made and demonstrate an understanding of low risk riding strategy
2.11	*Demonstrate a basic understanding of The Highway Code including 'who goes first', relevant road signs & lines*
2.12	*Decide where on and off road cycle infrastructure can help a journey and demonstrate correct use*
2.13	*Go straight on from minor road to minor road at crossroads*
2.14	*Use mini and single lane roundabouts*

Outcomes in italics are optional

You can make journeys on basic roads and are ready to use more complex roads

Level ③

3.0	Level 2 outcomes
3.1	Prepare for a journey: *route planning, weather, bike locking, night riding, and carrying bags and children*
3.2	Understand advanced road positioning turning on and off multi lane roads and roundabouts
3.3	Pass queuing traffic knowing when and how to filter
3.4	Demonstrate advanced hazard perception including (HGV) driver blind spots, and hazardous road surfaces
3.5	*Use traffic light controlled junctions including those with advanced stop boxes*
3.6	*Manage vehicles that pull in and stop in front such as buses when riding in bus lanes*
3.7	*Ride in pairs or groups and with other cyclists*
3.8	*Ride on roads with a speed limit above 30 mph*

Outcomes in italics are optional

You can ride on any road where cycling is allowed

2.
Becoming a Cycle Trainer

Here we will give an overview of the person specification of a cycling instructor to help you decide if the job is for you. We will outline the type of work you can expect and will describe the route to becoming a fully accredited National Standard Instructor (NSI). We will conclude this chapter with a list of the outcomes you must demonstrate in order to become a fully qualified NSI.

2.1 Am I the right person for the job?

Before beginning to train as an instructor:

You must:
- love cycling and wish to promote cycling as a serious form of transport
- be an experienced assertive rider whose main form of transport is a bicycle
- have a good understanding of The Highway Code and understand that people on bikes have the same rights on road as other road users
- have excellent communication skills and enjoy working with people of all ages

You should:
- have some experience teaching or coaching
- be of even temperament and friendly disposition, understanding the importance of acting professionally
- have some driving experience
- be able to check if a bike is roadworthy and know some basic bike mechanics
- be open to learn and develop as a cyclist and as a teacher
- be prepared to give and receive constructive feedback

2.2 How do I qualify as a NS cycling instructor?

4-day course

In order to become a fully accredited NSI and meet the specifications described above you will need to attend a 4-day instructor training course delivered by one of the Instructor Training Organisations (ITOs) recognised by the Department for Transport to award the NSI qualification.

These courses have a high practical element where you will examine your own riding and ensure that it is in line with the National Standard guidance. You will also explore the concept of risk management and apply the theory to practical situations. In addition to knowing the syllabus and how to manage risk you will learn how to teach and will practise teaching others on your course. You will write lesson plans and teach at all 3 levels of the NS. You will learn how to lead courses, manage groups and individuals, assess people's riding and learn how to offer constructive feedback. You will pass the 4 day course if you have managed to demonstrate a basic understanding of risk management, ability to communicate some parts of the syllabus and have demonstrated your own ability to ride to Level 3 of the NS.

Since on the course you only demonstrate teaching peers in role play situations your qualification is provisional (NSIP) until you demonstrate teaching real trainees in a Post Course Assessment (PCA).

Induction and mentoring

As an NSIP you are able to begin teaching. Ideally you will join a Bikeability scheme where you should be inducted and mentored while you find your feet and gain experience. (All Bikeability schemes should have an internal quality assurance system which will ensure you get help and support by more experienced instructors.) You will also need to consider first aid training, Disclosure and Barring Service (DBS) (previously called CRB checks), and insurance. If you plan to set up your own cycle training business as a sole trader you may wish to enlist the support of the ITO with whom you trained who would be able to offer mentoring services to ensure your first sessions are well delivered and low risk.

Post Course Assessment (PCA)

After you have gained some experience and within a year of the completion of the 4-day course you will need to be assessed teaching real trainees in order to be fully accredited. This should be done by the ITO that trained you initially (though it can be done through any ITO). It is better not to wait too long but to book your PCA after a few sessions. In most cases people require at least 2 PCAs to become fully accredited. The first PCA can be considered more like a mentored session where you receive feedback and action points about your teaching and risk management.

The PCA should take place ideally when you are teaching a session on road at NS Level 2 or 3 (not simply Level 1 control skills). It would be best if the PCA was of the type of work you usually do. So, if you are delivering Bikeability training to young people in a school, that should be the type of session on which you are assessed.

Throughout your training, from completion of the 4-day course until you are fully accredited, the ITO will notify the Department for Transport of your status. You will also receive a record of any action points you need to work on following the course and after each PCA. The ITO will also keep a record of any additional training or development you undergo and share that information (with your permission) with other ITOs should you wish to change the ITO you are affiliated to.

2.3 What work can I expect as an instructor?

a. Group training

The majority of work delivered by cycling instructors is teaching Bikeability to groups of young people in schools. This is currently partially funded by national and local Government. Some Local Authorities

partially fund adult group training. Groups of adults may also request training through their employer - many organisations will fund training as part of their responsibility for helping employees get to and from work safely. Adult groups may be funded through the National Health Service as part of an active travel campaign. Other group training includes driver training to help professional drivers understand how to share the road with people on bikes.

If you have good bike maintenance skills or have additional maintenance qualifications you could teach people how to fix bikes as well as ride them.

Other group activities include leading and marshalling mass rides for organisations.

b. Individual training

Some Local Authorities offer one-to-one training mainly for adults (and occasionally for young people). This training can often help people who wish to commute, yet are concerned about their skills, learn to ride confidently in traffic. There are surprisingly many people who have never learnt to ride and wish to take part in the fun. Getting an older person to ride independently for the first time is amazing and may mean that they are able to ride with their children or grandchildren.

There are individuals who have been advised by their doctor to get more exercise (cycling is probably the best form of non weight bearing aerobic exercise) and they require a session or two to remind them how to ride. Often during individual sessions your trainee will reach Level 3 of the National Standard. You may also help people plan their route to work or college. Such sessions are very dynamic, trainee progress is swift and they can be very rewarding.

2.4 What scope is there for career progression as a cycle trainer?

The sector has expanded as society values the role of the bicycle as a sustainable and benign way of getting around our cities. Cycle training looks set to stay. The sector has become more professional as demonstrated with the recent introduction of a quality assurance system.

A new instructor is expected to continually develop professionally, many schemes and most ITOs offer additional courses either refreshing skills or learning specialist training such as training for working with people with special needs; or training to run mass/ group rides etc. Some instructors may add additional qualifications such as bike mechanics training in order to offer maintenance training to people. Experienced instructors can train as mentors for their scheme and support new instructors to the sector. Across the country there are ITOs who need people (NSITs) to train new instructors. Cycle trainers often get involved in wider transportation and sustainability jobs and move into local authority jobs or transport consultancies.

Training as a cycle trainer can be a good start to someone's working life or an interesting and rewarding change in career direction.

2.5 What equipment will I need?

You will require these items for most training sessions:

- Roadworthy bike
- Tabard
- Mobile phone
- Basic toolkit (See p83)
- Maps and appropriate apps
- First aid kit (when you are qualified to use it)
- Trainee(s)/organisation/site contact details
- Diary for booking follow-up sessions
- Correct documentation (See 5.2)

2.6 The Instructor Standard

Here are outcomes that must be achieved (and assessed by your instructor trainer) over the 4-day course or during the Post Course Assessment (PCA).

1.	The National Standard & Bikeability	Course	PCA
1.1	Able to ride to Level 3 of the National Standard	✓	
1.2	Demonstrate an understanding of the structure of the National Standard and Bikeability	✓	
1.3	Demonstrate an understanding of: i) the concept of outcome based training ii) the progressive delivery of training, including increasing traffic and complexity through Levels 2 & 3 iii) the three levels, their outcomes and the importance of instructor/trainee ratios	✓	✓
1.4	Understand how the National Standard is delivered	✓	✓
1.5	Be aware of published 'all-ability' National Standard guidance	✓	

2.	Risk management	Course	PCA
2.1	Demonstrate knowledge or risk management relevant to cycle training - both formal (written) and dynamic risk assessment	✓	✓
2.2	Understand the 5 steps of risk assessment	✓	
2.3	Understand how and what to risk assess (trainee, bikes and environment)	✓	
2.4	Understand your duty of care, your responsibility for managing risk and know who to report to regarding risk management in your organisation	✓	✓
2.5	Assess risk dynamically during the session (using this as a teaching tool to aid trainees understanding)	✓	✓
2.6	Understand the principal areas of safeguarding children and vulnerable adults relevant to cycle training	✓	
2.7	Select appropriate areas for delivering the training appropriate to trainees' ability include alternatives in case their chosen site becomes unavailable	✓	✓
2.8	Write risk assessments of a variety of different training environments for Level 1 and Level 2 sites, listing any hazards and control measures	✓	✓
2.9	Demonstrate an understanding of emergency procedures and their importance	✓	
2.10	Assess at least one bicycle following a standard format (like the M-check) and fit a bike to a trainee	✓	✓
2.11	Identify and fix the following faults: i) low tyre pressure ii) loose or faulty brakes iii) loose attachments (wheels, racks, child seats etc)	✓	✓
2.12	Demonstrate moving a group of trainees between training locations by cycling on road (snaking) or walking where appropriate, and understand the advantages of moving groups on bicycles	✓	✓

3.	Communication, teaching and assessment	Course	PCA
3.1	Give clear instructions and demonstrate clear communication with trainees, other instructors and assistants	✓	✓
3.2	Give appropriate, positive feedback to trainees and check understanding	✓	✓
3.3	Motivate trainees to take part fully in the course	✓	✓
3.4	Use a variety of teaching techniques to suit different learning styles, judging which to use at key moments		✓
3.5	Manage trainees expectations		✓
3.6	Plan a session and a course and provide evidence of session plans for at least two outcomes from separate levels	✓	✓
3.7	Introduce a session, which should include: links to the previous session, initial trainee assessment, agreeing ground rules and setting aims and outcomes	✓	✓
3.8	Lead the delivery of at least two outcomes at each level, managing assistants where appropriate	✓	✓
3.9	Assess trainees at the start of the course ensuring activities and locations are appropriate to optimise learning	✓	✓
3.10	Manage groups ensuring trainees are under control and well behaved, dealing with any inappropriate behaviour		✓
3.11	Assess trainees during the course against the levels and outcomes of the National Standard giving ongoing feedback, knowing when to sign off outcomes once achieved with no input from the instructor(s)	✓	✓
3.12	Review and end a session giving clear feedback to trainees, their parents and course organisers/funders where appropriate	✓	✓

4.	Professionalism	Course	PCA
4.1	Behave in a professional manner on the course and while dealing with clients. This includes being punctual, dressed appropriately, and using appropriate communication	✓	✓
4.2	Make and keep effective training records, and use appropriate paperwork		✓
4.3	(optional) Direct trainees to appropriate resources and information that would enhance their enjoyment of cycling and make it more likely that they would choose to cycle	✓	✓

Don't forget that training progresses as your trainees get riding outcomes

You should not feel under any external pressure to complete levels within these minimum times

3.1 How long are courses and sessions?

The more time you spend with your trainee(s) the further you will progress through the syllabus. It is often the funding available that will dictate the length of a course. Most of the funded Bikeability courses are aimed at young people in years 5 and 6 of primary school where Levels 1 and 2 are taught to groups (though funding can be used for pupils up to year 9). Sessions should last at least 2 hours. Time can be eroded through poor logistics and lack of cooperation by the school. Good planning and communication with schools and individual trainees can minimise the risk of losing time.

Courses can take place over 4 or 5 weeks, 1.5 – 2 hours training delivered at the same time on the same day each week. This gives trainees time to practice skills and sort out bike problems between sessions. This model also maintains a longer term relationship between the cycle trainers and the schools and gives instructors a chance to promote cycling to the wider school community. This model may also enable instructors to do other work around cycle training if they have fixed days when they train. Courses can also take place over 4 or 5 consecutive days.

3.2 What are the instructor/trainee ratios?

All courses can be taught 1:1 where the best progress can be made through the syllabus and training can be targeted directly to the needs of an individual trainee. This is an ideal ratio for adult training and for complete beginners. Many working practices do not allow single instructors to work alone and therefore the ratios below may be multiplied to achieve the correct course size (e.g. 1:6 is 2:12 etc.)

3.3 Table of ratios and minimum course length

Level	Maximum number of trainees per instructor	Course time
1	1:15	2 hours
2	1:6 (2:12)	6 hours a. Level 2 course times can be scaled down where there are fewer trainees to a **minimum of 2 hours with 1 or 2 trainees** b. If there are more than 3 trainees per instructor they must be taught in 2 or more sessions and not delivered in a single day.
3	1:3 Where there are more than 2 trainees 2 instructors are recommended for busy Level 3 road environments	2 hours

4.
Ride Guide: Theory of National Standard Cycling

As a cycling instructor you will need to set an example to the people you teach. You will arrive at the session on a roadworthy bike that fits you and will be dressed appropriately for cycling. You will always demonstrate exemplary riding skills.

This section describes what you need to think about and do before you ride. It will also describe the National Standard riding style, starting with bike control off-road to using complex infrastructure. This manual will cover how to teach these skills in Part 6.

4.1

Level 1

Here you will learn how to ride off road and share off-road spaces with others.

> **1.1** Demonstrate an understanding of safety equipment and clothing and how clothing could make you more visible
>
> **1.2** Carry out a simple bike check including checking air, brakes, chain and direction of steering (ABCD)

a. Are you roadworthy?

You have eaten and are hydrated. You are wearing comfortable clothes appropriate for the weather. You are wearing gloves on cold days and have protection from the sun on hot days. You are carrying water in your pannier, backpack or water bottle holder on your bike. You may be wearing bright clothing especially if riding at night. Your shoelaces are tied and trousers are rolled up, tucked into your socks or you are wearing bicycle clips. If you are wearing a helmet it should fit snugly around your head and the straps shouldn't be loose under your chin. You may be wearing a cap to protect your eyes from the sun or rain.

b. Is your bike roadworthy?

Check your air. Make sure your tyres are hard. The recommended pressure is written on the side of the tyre. Riding on hard tyres will improve bike control and increase your speed, as well as minimise the chance of a puncture.

Check your brakes. Ensure that your brakes work well. Roll the bike forward and squeeze the front brake (right hand brake on most UK bikes). Roll the bike backwards then pull the back brake. The bike should stop sharply. There should be room to put two fingers between the brake lever and the handlebar.

Check your chain. Check that your chain is clean and lightly oiled and that it spins freely when you turn the pedals. It should be black or silver, not rust red. If it slips or makes a noise it may be worn.

Check your steering. To check that your handlebars are secured hold the front wheel between your knees and try to turn the handlebar. If all is secure the handlebars shouldn't turn.

Make sure your bike fits you. When you stand across the bike with your feet flat on the ground there should be at least 2" (5cm) clearance between your groin and the crossbar. Sit on the saddle and put your heel on the pedal. Your leg should be almost straight when the pedal is near the ground. You should also be able to reach the ground with the ball of your foot. You should not feel cramped nor too stretched out when holding the handlebar. Your fingers should be able to rest comfortably on the brake levers.

These are basic bike checks that every person who rides should be able to do. As a cycling instructor you will need to ensure that the people you teach are riding roadworthy bikes. You will need to be able to perform a thorough bike check and make some adjustments if required. (This will be covered in Section 5.5)

c. Controlling your bike

Your bike control skills need to be good enough so that when you are on road your attention will be focussed on what is happening around you rather than worrying whether you are in the correct gear or are able to look back and signal without wobbling. It is worth practising these skills off road until they become instinctive.

d. Getting on and off your bike

1.3	Get on and off the bike

Get on your bike from the left side. Pull your brakes before getting on and move the bike towards you lowering the saddle to make it easy to swing your leg over the saddle (or step through the frame) and sit on the saddle. Keep your brakes pulled while getting ready to go and when getting off.

e. Starting and stopping

1.4	Start off and pedal
1.5	Stop the bike

Set your pedal. Many people start with their right foot on the pedal and the left foot on the ground. Some start with their left foot on the pedal. Hook your foot under the pedal to get it to the start position (2 o'clock position for right foot/10 o'clock for left foot) where the pedal crank is in line with the down tube

Place the ball of your foot on the pedal. Start riding by pushing down hard with your starting foot and as the pedal comes around lift your other foot onto the pedal. Then keep pedalling. (If riding with toe clips

Cornering at speed

Consider raising the pedal on the inside of a turn. So if you are turning right raise the right pedal. This will ensure that the pedal doesn't clip the ground. Do this too where the surface slopes up when you are turning (called adverse camber). It is good practice to get used to doing this for all turns.

or cleats, clip in the starting foot before starting then clip in the other foot after one or two rotations.)

Stop the bike using both brakes and brace your arms; only putting your foot down after the bike has completely stopped. Stop with your starting foot on the pedal in the starting position so you are ready to go again quickly without having to reset your pedal. This can take some practice. (If you are riding a fixed gear bike or a bike with back pedal brakes, aim to time the stop when your pedal is in the starting position since on these bikes it is harder to set the pedal while stationary.)

f. Balancing, riding along and turning

1.6	Ride along independently (for at least a minute)
1.7	Make the bike go where you want

Balancing and steering are linked. To balance you need to steer the front wheel so you are constantly moving the bike back under yourself. (Balancing is not due to gyroscopic effects of the wheels spinning as is sometimes thought). This movement is unnoticeable in experienced riders. Beginner cyclists need to master this before they can make the bike go where they want it to so will keep changing direction while learning to balance. While riding, aim to keep pedalling (though freewheeling down a hill is one of the joys of cycling). Keep your head up and look in the direction you are going. Keep your fingers covering the brake levers so you are ready, at all times, to use the brakes for slowing down or stopping. Keeping your hand open and covering the brakes may also help relax your arm and neck muscles which will make looking behind easier.

g. Gears

1.8	Use gears (where the bike has gears)

Some people find the terms 'high gear' and 'low gear' confusing. If your feet are spinning too fast, (because you have increased your speed or are whizzing downhill) change up to a higher gear – This will be a higher number on the gear shifter. Likewise, if you are experiencing a lot of resistance and your pedals are hard to turn, change down to a lower gear (a lower number). There are a variety of shifting mechanisms. You may need to experiment to work out how to change gears on your bike.

Gear use helps you maintain a steady cadence (pedal turns per minute) whether you are moving quickly or slowly. A cycling rhythm is faster than a walking rhythm. The best way to increase pedalling cadence is to select a gear lower than the one you are used to. This may seem strange until your leg muscles adjust to using this increased rate of pedalling. Another advantage of getting used to riding in a lower gear is that of increasing the aerobic effect of pedalling which is good for your heart. A steady cadence (of around 80 revolutions/minute) should enable you to tackle most traffic situations.

A great advantage of good gear use is that of ensuring you are in a low gear when you start off - which ensures a speedy acceleration. If your bike has derailleur gears change down while pedalling whenever you need to slow down or stop. If your bike has hub gears, you are able to change gear while stationary.

If you ride a bike that has a front and rear derailleur, it is best not to be in a gear where the chain is on the largest chainring at the front and the smallest sprocket at the back, or a gear where the chain is on the smallest chainring at the front and the largest

High gear

Low gear

Gear use helps you maintain a steady cadence (pedal turns per minute) whether you are moving quickly or slowly

sprocket at the back. This is because the pressure you put on the chain in these positions when you accelerate twists and wears the chain, which could lead to your chain jumping when you try to change gear.

h. Emergency procedure

1.9	Stop quickly with control
1.10	Swerve to avoid objects

There are occasions while riding when you need to act quickly to avoid a collision. Being able to use techniques such as emergency stopping, swerving and even 'bunny-hopping' (lifting the front wheel over a hazard such as a pothole) may minimise the risk of crashing.

i. Emergency Stops

Normal braking involves using both brakes, slowing you down to a gradual controlled stop. Be prepared to brake at any time by riding with your fingers covering the brakes, with your thumbs underneath the handlebars, so your braking reflex will be slightly quicker. Emergency stopping happens more quickly than normal braking. When you pull either both brakes or only your front brake while moving fast, the front wheel locks, and the back wheel may lift off the ground and throw you over your handlebars. If you only use the back brake your bike may not stop, and your back wheel may skid, causing you to crash. To avoid this, aim to put as much weight as you can over the back of the bike. This helps both to prevent skidding and to stop your back wheel coming off the ground. Do this by bracing yourself by locking your arms - which will push you backwards. Stay seated on the saddle, perhaps sliding your bottom even further backwards if possible. You should also be able to push backwards with your feet if you have your pedals horizontal (level with each other). If your back wheel starts to skid, try 'pumping' the back brake by quickly releasing it then pulling it again to stop skidding. Once you have stopped, check behind, set the pedal, and start again when clear. You may wobble a little, since you may have had to stop in a high gear.

h. Emergency procedure

1.9	Stop quickly with control
1.10	Swerve to avoid objects

There are occasions while riding when you need to act quickly to avoid a collision. Being able to use techniques such as emergency stopping, swerving and even 'bunny-hopping' (lifting the front wheel over a hazard such as a pothole) may minimise the risk of crashing.

i. Emergency Stops

Normal braking involves using both brakes, slowing you down to a gradual controlled stop. Be prepared to brake at any time by riding with your fingers covering the brakes, with your thumbs underneath the handlebars, so your braking reflex will be slightly quicker. Emergency stopping happens more quickly than normal braking. When you pull either both brakes or only your front brake while moving fast, the front wheel locks, and the back wheel may lift off the ground and throw you over your handlebars. If you only use the back brake your bike may not stop, and your back wheel may skid, causing you to crash. To avoid this, aim to put as much weight as you can over the back of the bike. This helps both to prevent skidding and to stop your back wheel coming off

'Bunny-Hopping'
(This is not a National Standard outcome)

Riding into a pothole or a kerb may damage the front wheel. It is often enough to lift up the front wheel to get it over the lip of the pothole and avoid damage. To do this, relax your arms, drop your wrists below the bars, and push the handlebars up from below. This lightens the weight of the front wheel, and should be enough to lift it over the pothole or kerb. The rear wheel will follow through. (If you are using toe-clips or cleats you may be able to drop your ankles and push up your pedals, lifting the back wheel off the ground too.)

the ground. Do this by bracing yourself by locking your arms - which will push you backwards. Stay seated on the saddle, perhaps sliding your bottom even further backwards if possible. You should also be able to push backwards with your feet if you have your pedals horizontal (level with each other). If your back wheel starts to skid, try 'pumping' the brake by quickly releasing it then pulling it again to stop skidding. Once you have stopped, check behind, set the pedal, and start again when clear. You may wobble a little, since you may have had to stop in a high gear.

j. Swerving

Some hazards, such as potholes and glass in the road, are best avoided by swerving round them. While swerving, you move to the left or right of the hazard, then back into your original line. Keeping the arc of a swerve tight will prevent you from either crashing into the kerb on the left or veering into a vehicle on your right. The best way to swerve tightly and quickly is to use a technique called 'counter-steering'. Firstly, turn the handlebar towards the hazard, which moves your body away from the hazard, and then quickly turn the handlebar away from the hazard, moving the bike back under you and around the hazard. Using this technique will enable you to wiggle quickly around the object and back in line again in a tight swerve.

If you need to go over long obstructions such as tram rails, kerbs and pipes stretching across your path, approach them at right angles to avoid slipping along them.

k. Awareness and looking behind

1.11 Look all around including behind

You are almost ready to begin using your bike on road where you will need to be aware of other people using the road; some of whom will be behind you. Practise looking behind over both shoulders for a couple of seconds without wobbling. Ride in a straight line, when it's clear ahead, look back over each shoulder and challenge yourself to gather some information (such as the colour of the building behind you). If you find yourself wobbling, aim to keep your hands still compensating for your turn. Start by glancing back using only your neck muscles. Touch your shoulder with your chin to see further around. When you can do this and ride straight then try and stare behind longer, twisting your waist and shoulders.

You should be able to look back for different lengths of time. Learn to **glance** back, which is a brief look using peripheral vision enough to register nearby movement. A longer **scan** is achieved by twisting your torso and looking back long enough to get a complete picture of what is behind you. Taking a hand from the handlebar will enable you to turn more fully. There may be occasions where you need to **stare** behind (to communicate to a driver). This is a longer look where you will be twisting your waist, removing your hand from the handlebars and perhaps making a signal.

I. Signalling

1.12   Signal right and left

Before turning or changing direction you will need to signal clearly to people who need to know what you are planning to do. Always check behind before a signal. If turning left, glance over your left shoulder before raising your arm to signal. Signal clearly with your arm 90° from your body with your palm facing forward. Practise holding a signal for a few seconds.

It is worth trying to look back while holding a signal, this will help to ensure that the person behind you has seen and reacted to your communication when on road.

You will know that you are ready for the road once these control skills become instinctive. You will always start and stop with your pedal set. Cover your brakes. Change gear without thinking and glance back before sticking your arm out to signal. The next section covers the basic skills for sharing roads with other road users.

You will know that you are ready for the road once these control skills become instinctive

I. Decide when cycle infrastructure (both on and off road) can help a journey and demonstrate correct use

Off Road:

1.13	Share space with pedestrians and other cyclists

People are allowed to cycle in many parks, river and canal towpaths and on some pavements and other places where they can expect to share space with people on foot, with children playing and with dogs. People on foot always have priority.

Ride slowly passing people wide. While some people like to hear the ting of a bell from a rider wishing to pass others don't and prefer being asked politely. (Some people would rather cyclists kept to the roads and resent having to move constantly to let cyclists past.) Where there are many people walking consider

getting off your bike and pushing. Avoid intimidating walkers with fast or aggressive cycling. It is often a good idea to stick to the roads if you wish to get somewhere quickly.

When using a cycle lane separated by a barrier from the road check the surface for broken glass since these lanes may not be as well kept as the roads. The quality of separate cycle infrastructure varies; some may be too narrow for overtaking slower riders so you may need to be patient. Some separate cycle lanes may put you in less visible positions at junctions and force you to cross the road where drivers either aren't looking or expecting a person on a bike. Remember that you do not have to use such cycle infrastructure and may prefer to ride on the road. Some drivers may not understand why you are not using a cycle lane provided and may hoot you. There is some much better separate cycle infrastructure such as whole roads closed off to motorised traffic, provision of these is patchy.

4.2

Level 2

Here you will learn some basic principles for riding on road then explore specific manoeuvres giving you the skills and confidence to ride on basic roads.

See page 49 for all Level 2 Outcomes.

2.3	Be aware of everything around, including behind
2.4	Understand how and when to signal intentions to other road users
2.5	Understand where to ride on roads being used including when to ride in primary and when in secondary position

a. Ride assertively

Cycling assertively means asserting your rights as an equal road user:
- Being aware of who is on the road with you especially behind you.
- Positioning yourself where drivers can clearly see you ensuring they interact with you.
- Communicating your intentions clearly.
- Abiding by the rules of the road and knowing who has priority in any situation.

By being assertive you respect yourself and gain respect from other road users. You are and look confident.

Assertive does not mean aggressive. While the vast majority of drivers are ordinary people and don't wish to harm you, there are a few drivers who may not understand why you choose to position yourself in the middle of the lane and feel you are in their way. They may hoot or ride close behind you. Some may shout or swear at you. Avoid responding in a similar manner and remain calm (using only the hand signals mentioned in The Highway Code). If you genuinely feel at risk from a driver behind let them pass. Consider noting their registration number and report such anti-social driving to the police.

Cycling assertively means asserting your rights as an equal road user

More people are cycling and are riding assertively, and drivers are beginning to understand more about how people ride because either they are also cyclists or they have learnt from public information campaigns. Lower speed differentials between road users (like 20mph limits/zones) also help to improve interactions between drivers and cyclists.

Just like people on bikes expect respect from people in cars, cyclists need to respect the rights of other road users such as less experienced cyclists and pedestrians, giving way to them where appropriate and giving them space. While there may be some shared paths where cyclists are allowed to ride on the pavement, most pavement cycling, while not particularly risky, is illegal. It is slow and requires frequent stopping. Pedestrians are less disciplined and more unpredictable and the space is often limited. Pedestrians are often offended by adults using the pavement (though few object to young children doing this even though this is also illegal). Use the roads which is also not particularly risky and much more efficient.

b. Be aware of everything especially behind

Sharing the limited road space harmoniously means that we must all cooperate, by ensuring we are aware at all times. While riding concentrate on cycling. Pull over and stop to answer the mobile, check a map or have a drink, and avoid riding while holding anything in your hands which reduces your braking reaction.

Your eyes should be:

- scanning the road surface ahead looking for potholes, wet drain covers, black ice, debris and other hazards
- watching where you are going looking ahead, both sides and **behind**
- seeing what pedestrians are doing and other road users, spotting any parked cars about to move
- reading traffic signs, signals and markings
- checking around corners you are approaching and down roads you are passing
- checking between high sided vehicles when passing them
- making eye contact with drivers when you need to
- making eye contact with pedestrians and people on bikes where you may be in conflict with them

You need to know what is behind you at all times

In general it is much easier for people on bikes to see what is going on around them than people in cars who rely on mirrors for checking back. This often means that people in vehicles have spaces they are unable to see (blind spots). If you can't see a driver then they can't see you. Mirrors on bikes are not as effective as having a look back because the act of looking shows a human face to people behind and the movement of your head draws attention to you. The usual response to this eye contact is that drivers hang back or pass giving you more room. You need to know what is behind you at all times. You never want to be surprised by a driver passing who you didn't notice earlier.

There are different ways of looking behind.

A glance. This is a brief look back by just moving your head. Your chin touches your shoulder while your hands and torso remain in the same position. Regular glances will enable you to register what is just behind you, and will make drivers behind continually aware of you. You should do this while riding straight. You should also glance back just before changing position. This is called the 'lifesaver' or final check. Doing this will ensure you can react confidently in any unexpected situation. For example, if you encounter a pothole or other hazardous road surface, you will know if you can swerve to the right as you are aware of what is behind you.

A scan. This is done by twisting your head and upper body (and sometimes taking one hand of the handlebars) for long enough to get a fairly complete picture of what is happening behind. Use this before making any manoeuvre or before significantly changing speed. This will enable you to decide whether or not to signal or adjust your plan.

A stare. When you really need to make eye contact with someone behind, perhaps to prevent them overtaking, twist both your head and torso around taking your hand off the handlebar. You will be in good position to make and hold a signal while doing this. For a prolonged stare you will need to regularly glance ahead to see what is happening in front of you. A stare is useful to negotiate your way in front of someone approaching from behind when changing lanes.

Because of the importance of making eye contact consider wearing a peaked cap to shade your eyes rather than sunglass. A hood, your hair or anything else that limits your view behind should be arranged so you can see clearly.

While you should not ignore any of your senses **do not rely on hearing** for knowing what is around you. You cannot hear other cyclists, electric cars or pedestrians. While we do not recommend riding wearing headphones if you ever do and find yourself looking round more, this may indicate that you don't look round enough normally. People who have a hearing impairment are perfectly able to cycle.

c. Use road positioning to be seen

The Highway Code is not prescriptive about where cyclists should ride in the lane. It does, however, recommend that cyclists 'Leave plenty of room when passing parked vehicles' and 'take extra care near [road] narrowings'.

Take the lane where it would be risky to let drivers pass you

There are 2 main positions for cycling on road

The **primary position** which is in the middle of the traffic stream, often in the middle of a lane (but not always since traffic streams do not always stick to lanes). Riding in this position is also referred to as **'taking the lane'**.

The **secondary position** is just outside the traffic stream, to the left of it acting as a separate (narrower) traffic stream, yet riding close enough to be visible to drivers in the traffic stream. It is better to consider your position in relation to the traffic stream rather than in relation to the kerb.

How to carry items on a bike

3.1	Prepare for a journey: route planning, weather, bike locking, night riding, and carrying bags and children,

While riding a bike is a simple activity you do have to plan and decide what to carry and wear. You will also need to think how you carry a lock, some additional clothing, spares and tools. Some people prefer using panniers attached to their bike, while others like using courier bags and rucksacks. If you plan to be riding after dark you will need to carry lights. Avoid dangling bags from the handlebars and ensure any racks, lock brackets and child seats are firmly attached.

Primary position

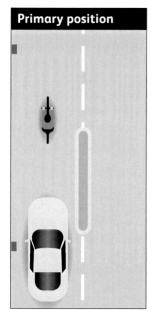

As its name indicates, the primary position is the default position to take. You are part of the traffic and are very visible to drivers because you are right in front of them. You are often doing drivers a favour by removing the decision from them whether to squeeze past you or not (though not all drivers see it that way). When in the primary position a driver will only overtake you when they are able to move into the oncoming (or next) lane, treating you as if you, too, were in a car.

You should to take the lane where it would be risky to let drivers pass you for instance when:

- passing a parked car (the driver could open the door without checking)
- approaching and moving through a junction
- waiting in a traffic queue
- the road narrows
- moving through a blind corner
- riding in a bus lane

Secondary position

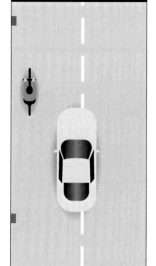

Drivers may beep you if you are in the middle of the lane and they do not understand why. A glance back as a smile may mollify them. You may decide to politely let them pass but avoid feeling intimidated and forced to move into a more risky position. Remember you are not blocking traffic, you are traffic.

Riding to the left of the traffic stream, in the secondary position, is a concession to road users coming from behind at higher speeds, allowing them to pass. Cycling in this position should be done only when it is safe to do so and generally not in the circumstances described above.

While riding in secondary position the distance from the kerb will depend on the width of the road.

Generally, **people overtaking will give you at least as much room to your right as you give yourself to your left**. If you are further away from the kerb and someone overtaking gets too close you still have room to move back towards the left. Avoid riding in the gutter where not only are there drains, potholes, broken glass and rubbish, you also have nowhere to go if someone gets too close. Always leave yourself a margin for error.

The less width available for the traffic stream the slower it moves. By moving right you can squeeze the traffic stream, slowing drivers down. This can be useful if you wish to move into the primary position. Whether riding in the primary or secondary position, good communication with other road users will help reduce potential conflict.

Regularly glancing behind while riding along not only ensures that you see what is behind you but also gets you seen by the people behind.

Ride predictably, develop a smooth riding line and avoid making sudden changes in direction and speed. Consider also the distance between you and a car in front. Drivers can stop their cars pretty quickly so avoid riding too close. If the traffic stream is slower than you, pass to the right (if there is room) moving early looking and signalling appropriately. In such circumstances it is often easier to ride to the right of the traffic stream where you can see round vehicles and others can see you are planning to overtake.

d. Communicate with other road users

People overtaking will give you at least as much room to your right as you give yourself to your left

When you ride assertively, look back a lot and position yourself where you are easily visible, you are already communicating well with other road users. In fact the more experienced you are at riding in this manner the less you need to actually signal. You should, of course, use clear hand signals (see 4.1.l) when you need to - they tell people exactly what you plan to do and they also draw attention to you.

Always look back before signalling - you can check whether anyone is there and needs to know what you intend and, much like signalling, it also draws attention to you. If no one needs to know what you intend (because either they are too far away to be affected or there is no one around - including pedestrians and other cyclists) then there is no need to signal. It is less risky to keep both hands on your handlebar. If someone does need to know your intention, signal before any manoeuvre so you have both hands controlling the turn. There is also no point in signalling while turning because it is clear to everyone that you are turning. (There is a view that you should always signal whether someone is there or not "just in case...". We advise against this since it moves the emphasis away from awareness and decision making to rote behaviour). Remember that signalling is a request which some drivers may ignore. Always check that a driver has responded (slowed down etc) to your signal before moving. Note too that some signals can be ambiguous such as when signalling right to overtake a parked car where there is a right turn ahead. A driver may assume you're moving to turn right and pull out in front of you. Timing of looking and signalling will improve with experience of different situations.

(Look back then) **signal right** when you plan to turn or move to the right, also signal right when you plan to remain on a road going right and people behind you may wish to turn off to the left (such as on a roundabout). This will deter a driver from overtaking them. In fact a right hand signal may prevent drivers passing you when you don't wish them to. When moving through a pinch-point in the road a right signal may be appropriate if you plan to move to a central position in the lane to prevent drivers overtaking.

(Look back then) **signal left** when you plan to turn left or are slowing and pulling over to the left.

The slowing down signal is hardly used now and may confuse people.

Use your head to communicate too. A nod and a smile to pedestrians crossing the road lets them know you're giving way to them. A flick of the head after glancing behind can let a driver know you are happy for them to overtake. (Avoid making overt beckoning signals with your hand in such circumstances since you shouldn't really be directing traffic).

Seeing, being seen and communicating are key skills for low risk cycling

e. Level 2 manoeuvres

We have covered the core principles of riding on road and are now going to apply them to different on-road manoeuvres as outlined at Level 2 of the National Standard.

2.1	Start an on-road journey
2.2	Finish an on-road journey
2.6	Pass parked cars and slower moving vehicles to their right
2.7	Pass side roads and crossroads riding along the major road
2.8	Turn right into a major road, do a U-turn then left into a minor road
2.9	Turn left into a major road and right into a minor road
2.12	Decide where on and off road cycle infrastructure can help a journey and demonstrate correct use
2.13	Go straight on from minor road to minor road at crossroads
2.14	Use mini and single lane roundabouts

f. Start and end an on-road journey

We ride on the left in the UK. Check right looking for any vehicles before putting your bike on the road. Start near the kerb where there are no parked cars or to the outside edge between parked cars, treating that position as the kerb. The key here is to start where you can be seen yet not obstruct traffic since people already moving on the road have priority (go first). Avoid starting too near junctions or on bends of the road where you will be less visible. Mount your bike, set your pedal and check over your right shoulder. Move off if there is no-one coming, and there is a big enough gap for you to move into without causing anyone to slow down or the traffic stream is far enough away that you can move into secondary position.

g. Pass parked cars and slower moving vehicles

If you are starting on a road that has cars parked on either side, move straight into primary position (See 4.2.c) which is at least a car door's width from any parked car. This will ensure you don't get hit by a car door should a driver open it without looking. It will also mean you are more visible to drivers behind and to pedestrians crossing the road between parked cars. Regular glances behind should ensure that drivers behind see you and may discourage them from passing you. As the vehicle in front you has priority drivers should remain behind until there is ample room to overtake. If you encounter a driver coming towards you neither of you have right of way so will need to negotiate, both you and they should slow down and pass where there is room to do this.

If you are riding in the secondary position and encounter a parked car you will need to take the lane, moving into primary position to overtake it. Plan ahead looking back early and assess the situation, move if clear. If there is a driver behind and you have room to move without affecting them signal your intention to move right then move. If you see a driver close to you consider waiting until that driver has passed before signalling. If there is a steady stream of

Overtaking parked cars

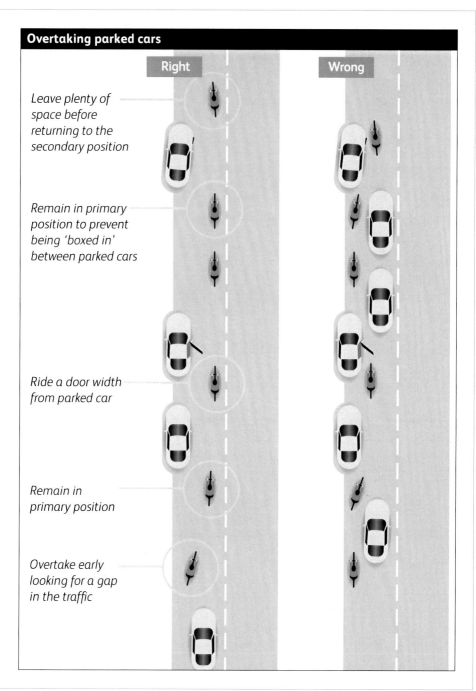

Right

Wrong

Leave plenty of space before returning to the secondary position

Remain in primary position to prevent being 'boxed in' between parked cars

Ride a door width from parked car

Remain in primary position

Overtake early looking for a gap in the traffic

motorists you may need to negotiate your way into the traffic stream. Looking back, making eye contact and signalling will often persuade a driver to let you in. The earlier you begin this negotiation the higher the chance you'll have of being let in. (If you are ever forced to remain in secondary position while passing close to parked cars, ride slowly and check for signs of drivers about to get out or pull out. Riding slowly will give you a chance to react).

After passing a parked car check over your left shoulder (looking for cyclists passing you on your left) before moving back to secondary position. Where there are gaps between parked cars it is often better to maintain your line on a road rather than weaving into the gaps. Moving into a gap may encourage drivers to pass, leaving you stuck behind a parked car. Remember that as the vehicle in front you do have priority over drivers behind and use the techniques described to minimise conflict with drivers.

h. Finish an on-road journey

To end a journey, choose a place away from a junction. You should be aware of what is behind through regular checks to the right while riding along. Check left (which communicates your intention to move left) and signal if anyone is there. Slow down and pull over next to the kerb. Dismount your bike straight onto the kerb.

Passing side roads

Cycle past a side road away from the junction

i. Pass side roads and crossroads travelling along the major road

People on a side road joining a major road should give way to people travelling on the major road. Give Way lines and the Give Way triangle signs indicate this. In order to give way, a driver on the side road will need to see what is coming on the main road. Where a road is parked up or where there is an obstacle obscuring a driver's view, drivers have to creep out of the side road in order to see. Unless there is a Stop Line (a solid white line, now quite rare) drivers do not need to stop behind the Give Way line. When a driver creeps onto the main road to see if there are vehicles on it, their car bonnet sticks out in front.

It is best to cycle past a side road away from the junction, often in primary position to ensure you get seen early by drivers in the side road and are well clear of the car bonnet. On approaching a side road, check right to see what is behind you, either maintain your line if riding in primary position (because of the parked cars) or be prepared to move to the right. This should not only get you seen by drivers in the side road, it will also prevent drivers behind overtaking while you pass a side road (where it is illegal to overtake). Look into the side road making eye contact with the driver so you know they have seen you. Look ahead for oncoming drivers who may wish to turn right into the side road. If cycling through a crossroad check into the road on the right too. Maintain your speed and keep pedaling so drivers won't think you're slowing down to turn.

Passing side roads

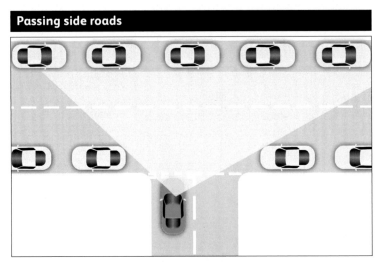

Drivers view behind the Give Way line at a T-junction obstructed by parked cars

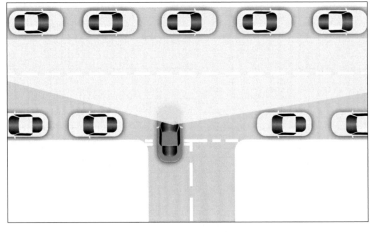

Drivers passes the line to get a clear view

Junction turns

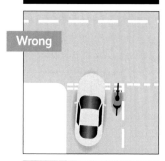

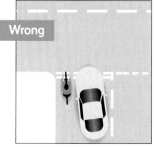

Avoid beeing 'squeezed' at the junctions

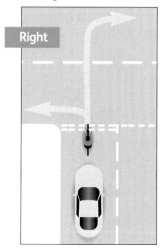

j. Turn right into a major road, do a u-turn then left into a minor road

As usual, planning any manoeuvre early makes it easier to manage. Check right in good time, signal if necessary and take the lane as you approach the junction for **the right turn**. Aim to reach the junction riding in the middle of the lane.

This will ensure that you have full control of the junction and drivers are forced to wait their turn as they should. If there is a vehicle already at the junction wait behind for your turn. Avoid moving too far to the right of your lane, to the middle of the road, where a driver also wishing to turn right has room to undertake you and force you into the oncoming lane as you turn.

As mentioned in 4.2.d you may not be able to see what is coming on the main road from behind the Give Way line so move to a position where you can see up and down the major road. If nothing is coming there is no need to stop but keep your momentum and make the turn. Give way to pedestrians at junctions who have right of way if they are crossing. If you do need to give way to a vehicle on the main road stop where you can see but are not impeding the traffic stream on the main road.

Do not cut corners when you turn. Doing so may tempt a driver behind to try and squeeze past you. Make wide sweeping arcs for all turns spending the shortest amount of time on the 'wrong' side of the road. Once you are on the major road check back to see what is behind you.

You can only do a **u-turn** when the road is clear in both directions since all other road users have priority. Ensure you perform a u-turn where you have good visibility ahead and behind so avoid doing this turn at a junction or a bend. Check ahead and behind. If anything is coming let them pass even if you need to pull over to the left and wait. When you are sure it is clear do a lifesaver check over your right shoulder just before turning.

Another u-turn method on a busy road is to remain in primary position or even, if there is space for drivers to pass you on your left, move to the middle of the road and perform the turn once there is a gap in the oncoming traffic. As usual after any turn check back to see what is behind you.

To **turn left from a major road into a minor road** check left before deciding whether to signal left or not. (You will of course be aware of what is on your right from your regular checks right). As with all turns you should move to primary position before turning to prevent drivers passing and turning across your path. Ride to where you can see, and be seen, by anyone in the side road, do a lifesaver check to the left then turn making the usual wide arc ensuring you are not cut up.

Planning any manoeuvre early makes it easier to manage

k. Turn left into a major road then right into a minor road

You will by now be used to the turning routine. For the **left turn from minor to major** take the lane at the junction and turn when there's a gap after the usual looking and signalling. Decide on your positioning on the major road prior to the turn and move into that position then the usual glance back to see what is there.

Turning right from a **major road onto a minor road** is often the most complex manoeuvre because you may have to cross a lane of moving traffic. The best way to handle this is to give yourself time by looking back and signalling (if necessary) early. If you are riding in primary position on the major road and the road is too narrow to be passed on your left, slow down and remain in the middle of your lane, drivers behind will have to wait (as they would if you were in a car). If there is room for you to be undertaken on your left, move to the right of your lane. If you do need to wait due to oncoming traffic, wait where you can clearly see up the minor road. When there is a gap have a quick look again over your right shoulder (the lifesaver) and turn into the minor road into the middle of the lane.

Left turn major to minor

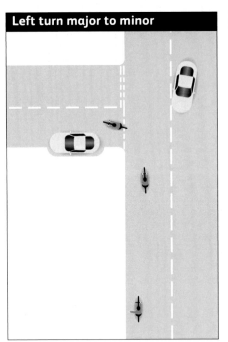

Left turn minor to major

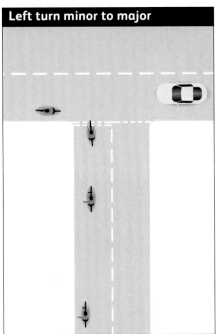

- Check behind a good distance before the turn – if there is traffic behind, signal left.
- Stop signalling just prior to the turn and with both hands on the handlebars, cover both brakes to control your speed.
- Look into the road you are turning into, checking for pedestrians, parked vehicles or hazards.
- Enter the road in the centre of the lane to prevent any following traffic from trying to pass you on the corner.
- Take extra care to control your speed on downhill turns.

- Check behind a good distance before the turn – if there is traffic behind, signal left.
- Turn or stop at the junction in the the centre of the lane. This prevents vehicles 'squeezing you at the junction'.
- If you have a clear view of the major road and you are positive there is no oncoming traffic – turn without stopping.
- If there is traffic on the major road – stop at the Give Way line.
- Check left and right, looking for a safe gap in the traffic.
- Turn and resume a suitable riding position.
- Make a quick safety check to the right as you turn out.

Right turn major to minor	Right turn minor to major
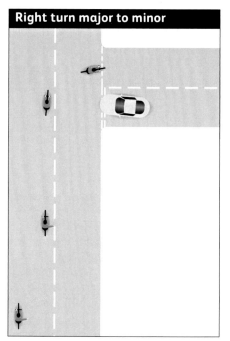	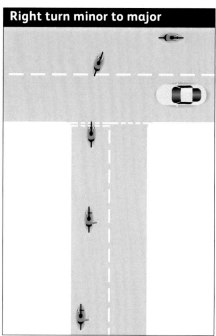

- Well in advance, check the speed and amount of following traffic.
- If there's a gap in the traffic, signal right and move quickly and smoothly to the left of the centre of the road.
- Check for oncoming traffic on the opposite lane.
- If there is no oncoming traffic, turn into the minor road.
- Make a 'lifesaver' look right before turning, to check you aren't being undertaken.
- If there is oncoming traffic, stop until it is clear to cross. Wait opposite the centre of the minor road. Take a last look behind before starting off again.
- Turn into the minor road in the primary position to prevent traffic trying to overtake you.

- Look behind early to decide if there is space to move to the centre of the lane. If necessary signal right.
- Turn or stop at the junction in the centre of the lane. This prevents vehicles 'squeezing you at the junction'.
- If you have a clear view of the major road and you are positive there is no traffic, turn without stopping.
- If there is traffic on the major road or your view is obstructed, stop at the Give Way line.
- Check right and left, looking for a safe gap in the traffic, then cross.
- Check right and left as you cross.
- Cycle the shortest route across the road – not a big arc.

I. Decide when cycle infrastructure (both on and off road) can help a journey and demonstrate correct use

On road cycle lanes:

You do not have to remain in a cycle lane and can choose to ride in the traffic stream if you deem that less risky or more efficient

Painted lanes on the road near the kerb may or may not be wide enough to use with minimum risk, they may or may not be clear of glass and debris and some may put you in less visible or risky positions such as too close to parked cars or junctions. (In London the Cycle Superhighways vary in quality and while they may be excellent for route-finding they are not always the best places to ride for the reasons outlined above). When riding in a cycle lane ride to the right of it away from the kerb to give yourself more space and room to manoeuvre. When cycling past side roads you may need to move out of the cycle lane to ensure you get seen by drivers creeping out of the side road. You do not have to remain in a cycle lane and can choose to ride in the traffic stream if you deem that less risky or more efficient.

m. Go straight from minor road to minor road at crossroads

When going straight ahead at crossroads move to the middle of the lane of the minor road you are using. (There is no signal for going straight ahead). When you have a gap in both directions cross into the middle of the new minor road.

n. Use mini and single lane roundabouts

(We will cover the principles of using of roundabouts in the next chapter (4.3.c)

o. Decision making and understanding The Highway Code

2.10	Explain decision making and demonstrate an understanding of low risk riding strategy
2.11	Demonstrate an basic understanding of the highway code including 'who goes first', relevant road signs & lines

Understanding the detailed manoeuvres described in 4.a-k, will ensure you are able to explain decisions you make on the road and will have given you a good grasp of low risk riding strategy. You will also have covered the points of The Highway Code regarding priority and have been introduced to some relevant road signs. You are now ready to begin Level 3.

4.3
Level 3

You are now a confident rider able to interact with other road users and use a variety of basic infrastructure on mainly single lane roads. You are now going to learn about using more complex multi-lane roads.

3.2	Understand advanced road positioning turning on and off multi lane roads and roundabouts
3.3	Pass queuing traffic knowing when and how to filter
3.4	Demonstrate advanced hazard perception including (HGV) driver blind spots, and hazardous road surfaces
3.5	Use traffic light controlled junctions including those with advanced stop boxes
3.6	Deal with vehicles that pull in and stop in front such as buses when riding in bus lanes
3.8	Ride on roads with a speed limit above 30 mph

a. Multi-lane roads

When riding straight along a multi-lane road you will generally use the left hand lane unless you are overtaking. If this lane is wide enough for you to be overtaken within the lane ride in secondary position. If it is too narrow to be overtaken within the lane, ride in primary position - drivers will have another lane to pass you. Since road widths vary you will need to claim the space you need by your road positioning. Be dynamic and adjust your position according to the circumstances. The lane markings are only a guide, decide in each situation how many traffic streams fit in the road space.

Should you wish to turn right off a multi lane road you will need to move across one or two lanes. Move a lane at a time. You need to plan early to give yourself enough time. Looking back and signalling at the same time will make your intentions clear to drivers. You position in the lane will depend on the lane width. If you do not have enough space to be passed within the lane, move from the middle of the left lane to the middle of the next lane. Drivers should understand your plan and some may slow to let you in front. If the lane is wide enough for you to be passed on the nearside, move to the right of the lane. (If the road behind you is completely clear then move diagonally, straight across all the lanes). Turn into the new road after the usual checks.

b. Bus lanes

In many places people on bicycles can share bus lanes with buses, taxis and sometimes with motor bikes. Riding centrally in a bus lane will ensure that you are visible and that bus and taxi drivers overtake you by moving into the next lane. If a bus is at a bus stop and signalling left overtake the bus using the procedure described above (4.2.g). Pass the bus wide out of the driver's blind spot and look into the driver's wing mirror. Passing wide will ensure any passengers exiting the bus and crossing the road on foot will see you early. If the driver is indicating right you should slow and let the driver pull away from the stop. You should move to the right of the bus so you can make eye contact with the driver in their mirror, perhaps nodding will indicate that you are aware and are giving way to them. When riding behind a bus (or any vehicle) hang far enough back to give you time to react if the bus comes to a halt. You should be able to anticipate when a bus driver intends to stop by being aware of bus stops ahead and the driver indicating. Slow down, check back then move to the right of the lane to pass.

taxi

Mon - Sun
At any time

You may be sharing the bus lane with other people on two wheels, some with and some without an engine. Be aware who is on your left by occasionally checking left. If you notice that a faster cyclist or motorcyclist wishes to pass you consider moving left to let them pass within the same lane so long as this doesn't put you in a more risky position (such as too near a junction).

Cyclist awareness training for drivers

More and more professional drivers are being trained to share the same space with people on bikes. Bus drivers learn how much room to give cyclists and when it's appropriate to pass. Drivers improved behaviour has minimised conflict in bus lanes, which makes bus lanes efficient places to cycle.

c. Roundabouts

The roundabout road is the major one-way road and the approach roads are all minor roads. This means you always give way to anyone already on the roundabout. When you are on the roundabout use the passing side-roads technique, making eye contact with drivers waiting to join the roundabout to ensure you are seen (see 4.2.i).

You should be in primary position on approach to and while using a roundabout, even if turning left. This will prevent drivers from squeezing past you and cutting you up, minimising conflict. It will also get you seen by drivers wishing to join the roundabout since you will be in the traffic stream which is where drivers check. (The riskiest, least visible place to ride is around the edge of the roundabout where you will be continually in conflict with drivers). A right hand signal will show drivers that you intend to remain on the roundabout. Look back and signal left after you pass the exit before the one you intend to use.

When using a multi-lane roundabout choose the correct lane on approach. If turning right off the multi-lane roundabout move into the centre of the right hand lane then move to the innermost lane spiraling left as you go round. Where there is more than one lane feeding into the roundabout the sight-line between you and a driver on the kerbside lane may be obscured by another vehicle. Make every effort to make eye contact with that driver.

The same principles apply to mini-roundabouts. Some drivers cut the corner and go over the central hump. You should avoid this. It contravenes The Highway Code and it may also be slippery especially when it's wet.

Roundabouts: Left turn

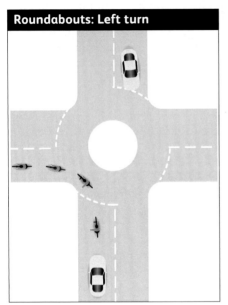

Roundabouts: Straight on

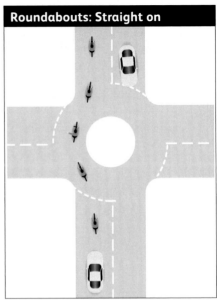

Roundabouts: Right turn

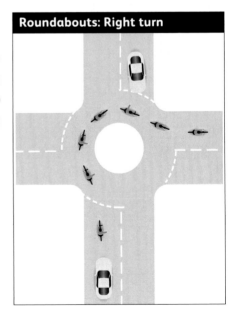

Make eye contact with drivers waiting to join the roundabout to ensure you are seen

d. Filtering

One of the advantages of being on a bike is the ability to move past a traffic queue. This is called filtering. It is often more efficient and less risky passing a traffic jam to the right. This is where drivers expect to be overtaken so will generally check right before turning. You will also have less conflict with pedestrians stepping off the kerb and will have more room especially if the oncoming lane is empty (which may be the case if the traffic is stopped at lights). Whether or not to filter will depend on how long you anticipate waiting. If the traffic slows briefly and you can see that everyone will move again in a short time consider waiting in the traffic stream.

If you notice the traffic slowing move to the right of the vehicle in front of you so you can see whether there is room to filter. Look back checking for motorcyclists and faster riders. Pass the traffic queue slowly watching out for people on foot stepping out between vehicles in the queue. Be especially aware when passing a large vehicle. It is often possible to ride away from queuing drivers especially if the oncoming lane is empty. If, while filtering, you see a driver coming towards you on the oncoming lane, move left. It is possible to wait at a 'station' between two queuing cars until the vehicle has passed them, then continue to filter.

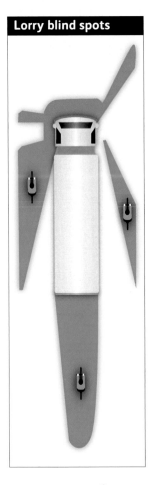

Lorry blind spots

e. Lorry driver blind spots

Much is being done to improve the interaction between lorry drivers and cyclists including fitting additional mirrors both in the cabs and at junctions and installing proximity sensors to detect if a rider is near the lorry. There is only so much that can be done using technology and drivers have only one pair of eyes. Be aware of places around a lorry where drivers are unable to see.

principles such as, passing traffic queues wide and to the right, and ensuring you make eye contact, should minimise the risk when sharing the road with lorry drivers. **Never pass down the left side of a lorry**. Be aware that some articulated lorries need to swing right before turning left.

f. Traffic lights

Green means go. All other combinations mean stop. On approaching a red light move into primary position and stop behind the stop line. If turning left or right and there is a filter lane move into the middle of the appropriate lane.

If there is a queue at a red light decide whether to wait your turn or to filter towards the front. If you think you can get through the lights in one change of lights it is often better to wait in the queue. (One downside of doing this is that you may be directly behind a car exhaust emitting fumes). Should you decide to get to the front, pass on the right as described in 4.3.d. In some circumstances there may be enough room to pass on the left. Since it is illegal to cross the stop line when the light is red wait behind and to the right of the first car in the queue signalling to the driver in the second car that you intend to join the traffic stream when the lights

Be aware of places around a lorry where drivers are unable to see a cyclist

change. If the lights change while you are passing the queue you should be able to move left into the traffic stream as the drivers move off. You will notice a concertina effect as each driver waits for the one in front to go before moving. Good eye contact and signaling should ensure you are able to move into a space.

Some traffic light junctions have an advanced stop box or advanced stop line (ASB/ASL) so cyclists can position themselves ahead of the traffic. Some have feeder lanes to the left which send a mixed message encouraging riders to filter left. This can be risky for reasons already discussed. You do not have to use these filter lanes. Position yourself centrally in the ASL in front of the traffic and remain in the primary position as you move through the lights. Only move into secondary position to let drivers pass once through the lights and there is no other reason for you to remain in the primary position.

g. Riding on roads with speed limits above 30mph

All the principles described remain the same, when cycling with high speed traffic. You will need to adjust your timings when manoeuvring giving yourself more time to move. On some occasions where you may wish to turn right across a few lanes of fast moving traffic you have the option to dismount and cross on foot using a crossing.

h. Riding in pairs

3.7	Ride in pairs or groups and with other cyclists

You are allowed to **ride side by side** with other cyclists. The Highway Code advises you not to ride **more** than 2 abreast. Riding side by side can be pleasant and sociable and in many situations lowers the risk of riding even more by making you more noticeable. However in towns people in cars may feel inconvenienced when driving behind two chatting riders so riding in single file, even if doing so in primary position, may cause less conflict. Knowing who else is on the road with you may enable you to decide dynamically when riding side by side is appropriate and when it isn't. If you are riding next to another rider ensure you give each other enough swerving room. If you a riding to the right of your friend, give them room to ride away from junctions and parked cars.

Riding one behind the other is a useful technique to buddy a new cyclist or for a parent to ride with their child. If you are buddying a novice rider or a child ride behind them slightly to their right where you can protect them and communicate with them. (We will explore techniques for moving individuals, pairs and groups of riders on road in Part 8).

Riding in the manner described in this section takes some practice. You will need to be a 'Level 3 cyclist' and ride in this way instinctively to set a good example to your trainees and to demonstrate good practice. As you train to be an instructor you may find you have developed some bad habits over years of riding that you will need to undo. If anything happens to you while riding such as getting cut up - ask yourself if you could have done anything different. You never stop learning to ride a bike. Being self-aware and honing your technique will increase the pleasure you get from riding and the enthusiasm and skills you will be able to share with your trainees

"The skills that I learnt from my training has made riding more fun and helped me feel more confident"

5.
Managing Risk

A core element in the job of a cycling instructor is minimising risk for all activities. Like any area of expertise, you will become more adept at identifying hazards and minimising risk the more experience you gain. (Which is why your initial accreditation will be provisional while you work with experienced instructors to gain expertise in this area). Your trainees also, will gain knowledge and understanding of how to minimise risk while riding a bike from you during the training.

5.1 Risk assessment

'Risk' means the likelihood of harm and is measured as a percentage chance of something bad happening or more simply described as high, medium or low risk. Possible causes of harm are called 'hazards'.

We learn throughout our lives how to manage risk and the risk assessment thought process is natural to us. Typical sequence of events might be:

- Observe and identify potential hazards (**Identify**)
- Assess whether the hazard poses significant risk (**Assess**)
- Act to remove, minimise (or protect people) from the hazard (**Remove**)
- Record what you have done (if appropriate) (**Record**)
- Review by keeping vigilant (**Review**)

5.2 Duty of care

You have a 'duty of care' for everyone involved in the training so will need to apply this thought process to the people involved (trainees and other instructors and yourself), their bicycles and equipment, and the training environment (on and off road). You will be expected to use this thought process formally by filling in forms which prompt you with what to consider prior to training. These documents will include:

- A consent form/risk assessment for everyone you train
- Register for groups of trainees
- Off road site survey
- Road survey for training sites and routes
- An incident reporting form

Dynamic risk assessment recognises the fact that things can change

The requirement to manage risk during the training is at least as important as formally assessing risk prior to the training session. This is dynamic risk assessment which recognises the fact that things can change. When something happens that increases the risk you need to notice and act immediately. In the next section we are going to explore what you can do to minimise risk before and during the session for the trainee, their bike and the environment. While we are mainly focusing on the people you are training remember that you have a duty of care for everyone involved including other instructors and assistants and yourself.

Before training

Any information you can find out about your trainee or group of trainees in advance of the session will help you minimise risk.

You may receive some information about individual trainees when being booked for work by email. You can also speak to them a few days before the session (we call this a 'checking call'). You can find out about their aims and previous cycling experience (including notes on previous lessons), any concerns they may have, any health and fitness issues, and if they have any special needs. You can discuss with them what they can expect, what they should consider wearing and agree the details of the meeting location and time, and how you will identify each other. When you meet them you will get their consent (or their parent's consent), their next of kin's contact details in the unlikely event of an emergency and formally fill in a risk assessment form.

5.3 Your trainee(s)

You may have less information about groups of school pupils prior to a course. It is worth asking teachers if they can point out pupils with any special needs or relevant health issues. You should also receive a consent form from parents or guardians of pupils which should give you some information to help your risk management. Keeping a record on a register for the whole group will make it easier to monitor risk and note any issues. Use the register to record their progress through the syllabus during the course.

During training

On meeting your trainee(s) check that they are dressed appropriately for riding - their shoelaces are done up and baggy trousers tucked in, they are not wearing a hood which may obscure their view and anything else dangling is removed. Watch out for any changes during the session.

Keep an eye on your trainee's health and fitness. Some people may need to take breaks if they are not used to exercise. Ensure they are hydrated and have eaten so they have the energy to do the training. If they need any medication (such as an inhaler) you need to know and make sure they have it with them. On sunny days ensure they have appropriate sun-protection, and on cold or wet days that they are dressed for the weather. Work through the syllabus at their pace. This means that the challenge should be just right. Remember, there is an element of risk involved if they are not challenged enough, especially when training groups of young people who may get bored and misbehave. You or your co-instructor will need to ensure you can see your trainees at all times during the session. And don't forget to ensure that both you and your trainee(s) are enjoying the session which will keep everyone focussed and learning well.

You or your co-instructor will need to ensure you can see your trainees at all times during the session

5.4 The environment (site and route assessment)

Level 1 - off-road site survey

Complete beginners

Before training

You will need to visit the training location and ride the route you plan to use to get your trainees to the location before the session. It is a good idea to visit the location around the same time that you plan to run the training in order to assess the conditions. While it is tempting to choose fixed sites in advance you may wish to vary these once you have met your group or trainee. Remember that conditions can change so have plan B routes and locations. Outlined below are the site requirements for different types of session.

Off-road wide tarmaced space such as an unused car park, basketball or tennis courts are suitable for complete beginners. These are 1:1 sessions, however the trainee needs plenty of room.

Off-road groups and individuals

For groups, a similar site to the beginner site mentioned above with enough room for up to 15 people to ride together. For individuals it is possible to use park paths or even very quiet roads/dead ends to teach and assess their bike control skills.

In addition to the size of the off road site, note the surface condition - looking for debris, glass, puddles, and slippery mossy sections etc. Check if other people or animals are using the space, what amenities are accessible such as toilets and water, and any other hazards. Record any actions you have taken (such as cordoning off a slippery area) on the site assessment form.

Levels 2 & 3 - on-road site and route survey

> The locations for training must be appropriate to the riders skill level

School groups

You will need to find locations within an appropriate distance from the school depending on the ability of the group. You should expect to run no more than 2 or 3 activities at 2 or 3 locations per school session of around 2 hours. It may be appropriate to find locations near the school if time is short, though it is often better to ride with trainees away from the school catchment area so the young people learn how easy it is to go some distance on a bike. A new area also takes them away from their home territory where there may be some local distractions. As well as the infrastructure matching the outcome you hope to achieve, the locations for training must also be appropriate to the riders skill level. Traffic density will increase as you go through the syllabus to give trainees more and more opportunity to communicate with other road users. Lines of sight must be good so instructors can observe trainees at all times. There must be room for trainees to stand and observe the road and somewhere to park their bikes close to the location. Minimise the chance of getting bikes stolen by stacking or locking them if required. Choose places where you are not going to damage people's property such as fences and hedges, and ensure other people can use the pavement without being blocked. You will also need to check the road surface and markings.

As you will learn when you read the section about 'snaking' (Chapter 8), it is possible to move a group of trainees who have great bike control skills in Level 3 environments such as in bus lanes on A-roads. If planning this type of group move, ride the whole route and note places where you may find it easier to get off the bikes and use a crossing. Consider avoiding right turns which can be more complicated and check out the traffic density since when moving a group you won't be filtering

through traffic and may end up stuck in a traffic jam. Consider including a site of local interest along the route for added fun! Record the route you plan to ride (or walk) with your group on the road/route survey form and include plan B routes.

Individuals

You can be more flexible finding locations for individual sessions as these can be more dynamic and you are able to move quickly from site to site. Your trainee may have specific locations they plan to use. Scout out an area prior to the session near their home or the park where you will be meeting them, and have a few options. For individuals looking to commute by bike you may end up accompanying them on their route to work. Be prepared to find Level 3 locations (but only move to Level 3 when they are very confident at all Level 2 activities.)

During training

Remember that things may have changed! There may be people playing football on your Level 1 location, it may be locked, be icy or waterlogged. You will need to decide whether you can use an alternative. You may even need to call off the training based on your risk assessment.

Pehaps your on-road location may be busier than expected for example during the school run or refuse collection. Use your plan B. It may be that you find an even better site on the way and decide to use that. During the training you or your co-instructor are continually scanning the pavement and road - ensuring trainees aren't blocking the pavement and checking to seeing if the road conditions have changed and how that will impact on the activity (such as a van blocking visibility).

5.5 The trainee's bike and equipment

Before training

When you meet your trainee(s)you must check their bike and equipment as described below. In order to minimise the risk of them turning up with an unroadworthy bike discuss their bike's condition with them beforehand. It is a good idea to email the trainee information describing a roadworthy bike/basic bike check. You may also wish to find out their bike type which may help you plan your session more effectively. You can train people on any road legal bike as long as you accommodate any limitations (such as a single speed bike whose rider may struggle up hills) in your planning.

It is a good idea to email your trainee information describing a roadworthy bike and a basic bike check

The bike check

On meeting your trainee or on having access to their bicycle you need to check it thoroughly. It is a good idea to check a group of trainees' bikes outside a school session so time isn't taken from the training. (You will also need to teach trainees how to check their own bike which we cover in Part 7.1)

The better your bike maintenance skills the quicker you will be able to check and adjust bikes, and, depending on the tools you carry (see below), the more bikes you will be able to include in the training. You will need to understand when a bike must be excluded from training if you are unable to adjust something, such as when a brake doesn't work; and when you can include a bike even though there is problem, such as when a spoke is missing.

Check that your trainee is happy for you to make adjustments before doing so. If based on your risk assessment you deem a trainee's bike unfit for riding you will need to explain this to them, (if on a school's

Fitting a helmet

A helmet should fit snugly around the head, be horizontal and cover the upper part of the forehead. The straps should form a V-shape just below the ears. Use the front straps of the V-shape to adjust the helmet and pull it forward and the rear ones to adjust it pulling it backwards. The straps should be done up under the chin so two fingers can just be squeezed between the strap and your trainee's chin. Remove their helmet before making adjustments to avoid touching them or pinching their skin.

Wrong   Right

course write a short note to their parents) and to advise them to go to a bike shop. Keep a record of any adjustments you make.

Fitting a bike to the trainee

You will need to get your trainee on their bike to check whether it fits them. Ensure that they pull their brakes while they get on and off. Check the frame size by asking them to stand over the crossbar with their feet flat on the ground. There should be 2 inches clearance between them and their bike. When seated on the saddle they should be able to reach the handlebar without stretching. While the trainee shouldn't be too cramped it is risky to ride a bike where the frame is too big. The saddle height should be set to where they can reach the ground with the ball of both feet. Put the pedal at the lowest position and their heel on the pedal. Their leg should be almost straight. (Consider putting the saddle slightly lower than the optimum position for complete beginners so they have confidence they can reach the ground). Handlebar height can vary depending on how aerodynamic a person wishes to be. Brake levers need to be positioned so your trainee has straight wrists when covering their brakes and they can easily reach the levers.

During training

While training keep monitoring trainees' bikes. Observe how they are braking and how they are handling the bikes. Do they look comfortable and in control? Do the bikes sound fine with no strange rattles or noises? Are gear changes smooth? If in doubt ask the rider to stop and recheck their bike.

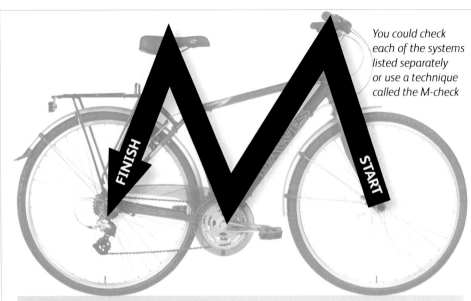

You could check each of the systems listed separately or use a technique called the M-check

FINISH

START

List of checks you should make:

Wheels
- Tyres pumped up
- Tyres not split, cracked or bulging
- Axle and cones not loose and wheel spins freely
- Rim not bent or damaged
- No missing or broken spokes
- Valve is straight

Brakes
- Blocks not worn away
- Blocks touch rim squarely not tyres
- Brakes stop bike and are not loose
- Blocks release quickly
- Cables not frayed

Transmission
- Pedals and cranks turn freely
- Bottom bracket not loose
- Chain oiled with no stiff links
- All gears work and changing is smooth

Frame
- No cracks or damage to frame
- Headset spins freely and is not loose
- Seat-post and handlebars below maximum insertion line
- Saddle and handlebars are straight and can not be moved out of alignment
- Bar ends plugged

Accessories
- Reflectors and lights fitted appropriately
- Mudguards, racks, locks, child-seats fitted securely and correctly
- Helmet not damaged or dented and the right size

5.6 Dealing with emergencies

In the same way that riding a bike is a low risk activity so is cycle training because you will be acting at all times to minimise risk. In this section we look at what you need to do if anything does happen such as if a trainee falls off their bike while riding with a group on road. Here is the procedure for managing such emergencies. Use other instructors and members of the public to help if necessary:

1. Stop the activity and ensure no one is in imminent danger
2. Assess the situation calmly
3. Administer first aid if required
4. Call the emergency services dialing 999 (or 112) if required
5. Contact your manager and/or the school (so they can contact next of kin)
6. Reassure the rest of the group letting them know what is happening
7. Remain with the injured person until the ambulance arrives. The paramedics will take over your 'duty of care' for the injured person so you can focus on getting the group back to base.
8. Record details of any witnesses and numbers of other vehicles involved. Take pictures/sketches of the scene
9. Follow your organisation's guidelines for incident reporting including filling in an incident report

As you gain more experience teaching cycling your ability to preempt problems and nip things in the bud will get better as will your ability to adjust elements of your training to suit your trainee and minimise risk.

Basic tool kit

This is the minimum requirement for any cycle training session. Should you be running a Dr Bike or other maintenance course you would of course require additional tools, spares and parts.

- Spanner set: (15mm, 13mm, 10mm) or adjustable spanner
- Set of Allen keys or multi-tool
- Screwdrivers: flat head and Phillips
- Pump with Presta and Shrader valve attachments
- Puncture repair kit/ spare inner tubes

6.
Teaching and Learning

Communicating the syllabus to your trainees clearly and enthusiastically while giving them a lot of time riding their bikes and improving their skills is key to a good session.

In this section we will explore different ways people learn and how to manage groups keeping everyone engaged (including people with special educational needs). You will learn how to structure any teaching session to include theory, demonstrations and a variety of riding activities, and how to evaluate learning and give feedback.

6.1 How do people learn?

Learning preferences

People learn in different ways. Simply put, people may be auditory (listening), visual (observing) or kinesthetic (moving/doing) learners. In fact most people use all three although one mode may be dominant. Cycling is a practical activity, the majority of learning happens while people are riding therefore a training session should involve a lot of riding. When teaching a group of young people, it is good to cover all types of learning preferences by asking, telling, and demonstrating to the trainee, before getting them on their bikes. It is worth being aware of your own learning preference since you may prefer teaching the way you learn (so if you are an auditory learner you may tend to tell rather than show demonstrations). Self awareness of this may ensure you mix up your teaching to cover others' needs.

Asking questions

People also learn when they are involved in the session and interacting with the instructor and others in the group. Using a series of structured questions will keep trainees involved and thinking. Questions will also give feedback to you that they understand, as well as create opportunities to reward trainees with praise when they get answers right.

Using **open questions** (which have many answers) to introduce a topic will ensure that trainees can be involved from the outset and have their answers (more than one) rewarded e.g.When may you need to do an emergency stop? **Leading questions** elicit specific answers which help develop your trainees understanding e.g. Who goes first at a T-junction,

Open questions: (many answers) elicit many answers, which helps introduce a topic to trainees

Leading questions: (one answer) elicit specific answers, which help develop your trainees understanding

people on the main road or the side road?) Before they have a go doing the drill a quick **checking question** will indicate to you that they have a basic understanding of what to do. This helps minimise risk. A checking question may be a repeat of an earlier question e.g. Where do I stop at this junction?

Demonstrations

You must demonstrate everything before getting your trainees riding. Ensure that the whole group can see the demo. Use questions to keep them involved while watching. You could set a task such as asking them to note two things the rider (generally your co-instructor) is doing well and two things they could do better while riding. Such a task may involve using a bad or mixed demonstration with some good and poor riding techniques. This is fine as long as just before your trainees ride they see a good demonstration. (Consider using a trainee with good skills to demonstrate as it may help keep the group interested in the session.) If teaching by yourself ensure trainees are standing in a safe place where they can see your demonstration. If many of your trainees make the same mistake when riding show them again as well as tell them to ensure different learning preferences are addressed.

Young people can have a short attention span so changing activities and delivering a pacey session may help to keep them focussed and involved. This will also help with group management (See section 6.2). Having a varied up-paced interactive learning experience with lots of practical riding is also much more fun than passively listening to someone deliver a lecture.

Understanding your trainee's aims and learning about their riding experience will enable you to pitch the session appropriately.

Who goes first?

It is possible to introduce some more technical language to your trainees by teaching them what such terms mean in a simple manner. So asking them 'Who goes first?" at a T-junction is an opportunity to introduce the concepts of 'priority' and 'give-way'. Once your trainees have demonstrated that they understand the term 'priority' it is possible to use that for the remainder of the course.

Mind your language

Pitch the language you use according to the level of understanding of your trainees. While it is good to increase their vocabulary, check their understanding with some simple questions. You need to decide with each group and individual where to pitch the language. With some people you can refer to primary/secondary position or decide to simplify these concepts by talking about being in or out of the traffic stream. If you are teaching adults, especially if they can drive, you should use more technical terminology so they don't feel patronised.

Remember that the main aim of training is to encourage people to ride their bicycles. Training for many people is about building up their confidence and helping them manage their fear. Helping them understand that riding assertively will ensure drivers see them is much more positive than telling them that if they ride where they are less visible they are likely to get knocked off. Avoid using scary language such a 'dangerous' or suggesting that they may get injured or harmed. Overuse of the word 'safe' conjures up 'danger' and can be less helpful than defining what you mean by safe. For example saying: "Start when it's safe to go" is much less informative than saying "Start when there is a gap in the traffic".

Can the car see the bike?

As a society we are guilty of depersonalising road users and personalising inanimate objects especially cars. It is absurd to say 'The car can't see you from this position' or 'check if a car is indicating'. Refer to people, drivers, people in cars, people on bikes etc. Ask trainees "To make eye contact with drivers". Avoid using the word 'accident' which removes responsibility from the person driving carelessly. Use the word 'crash' or 'collision' (The police no longer use the term accident and prefer crash or incident.) It is also worth distinguishing between a crash and a fall which occur in very different circumstances, falls often don't involve another person.

We don't 'assume everyone else is an idiot' nor do we suggest that people on bikes should 'assume they are invisible'. The opposite is the case. We teach people to ride where others see them and to communicate clearly, checking they have been seen. We teach people how to pre-empt conflict and how to avoid hazards. Through training people learn to cooperate with other people on the road by ensuring they get seen and are aware of other road users and that clear communication and courtesy is key to minimising risk while sharing the same space.

> The manner in which you begin a course will dictate the tone of the rest of the course

6.2 Managing groups

A positive interactive teaching session with varied activities and delivered at a good pace will go a long way in ensuring that trainees are well behaved and focussed throughout. In this section we will explore some additional techniques that should help contribute to getting good learning outcomes and progressing through the syllabus.

Communication

Consider what you are communicating to your trainees. You need to ensure that you look and sound confident, are in control, have a plan and are enjoying yourself. From the start of the first session and at the beginning of each subsequent session gather your trainees around you in a semi-circle so they can all see you. You should speak calmly and confidently and make eye contact with them and use open approachable body language and smile. If you are clearly enjoying teaching them they are more likely to enjoy learning.

The role of a co-instructor

For most group courses you will have a co-instructor (or an assistant instructor - NSAI) who will help with teaching and group management. You and your co-instructor will have made a plan and agreed who does what in advance of the course. The co-instructor will help with group management and aim to diffuse any situation while you are teaching (for example that might mean having a quiet word with a trainee to help them focus). The co-instructor may also demonstrate techniques while the lead asks questions. In some circumstances, at Level 1, the co-instructor may work with an individual or small group of trainees to help them catch up or work on skills with a view to integrating them back into the group at a later time. The co-instructor should be involved in teaching, perhaps alternating with the lead so trainees have varied input and teaching styles. The co-instructor has a major role in moving groups around on road (See Chapter 8) . They may also be helpful in guarding bikes if there is a need for the group to wander away from the bikes to observe something.

Group discussions

Wrong

Wrong

Right

Aims and expectations

Introduce yourself and your co-instructor telling them your first names.

Start by discussing with your group the aims of the course. Tell them that the aim is to learn skills to help them ride on roads. Explain the course structure so they understand that they will start by looking at what they need to think about before riding, such as what to wear, and know how to check their bike. They will then have some fun, playing games in the playground improving their bike control skills before going on road. Find out what riding experience they already have and contrast any experience they may have such a mountain biking or BMX riding with road riding.

Learn their names

It is basic respect to learn everyone's name from the start of the session so make a special effort to do this. Not only is this going to help build their trust in you it will also help manage risk and enable you to target questions at specific individuals who may be distracted.

With the group clustering in a semicircle in front of you, where they can all hear and see, you ask the first person (e.g. the person furthest left) to tell you their name. Then ask the name of the person next to them and repeat the list of their names backwards, saying them out loud. If you don't catch a name get them to repeat it.
For example:
'Davide'
Sheherezade.
'Sheherezade, Davide'
Kelly
'Kelly, Sheherezade, Davide'
Suliman
'Suliman, Kelly, Sheherezade, Davide'

Once you and you co-instructor have learnt the names begin using them while asking questions to ensure you remember. If you forget a name ask them again. You will, of course, have collected a consent form for each trainee and have a register. It is a good idea to ask your co-instructor to check the consent forms and write names into the register while you are introducing the session or copy the names into the register outside the session so you begin the session on a high rather than with a form filling interaction.

Ground rules

> Keep ground rules simple and brief and coin them in positive language which will set the tone for the course

Once you have learnt their names you need to agree how you expect the group to interact with each other. Ask them what we can all agree on that will ensure everyone gets on and works well together. Most young people will be used to this and are likely to come up with these ground rules:

- One person talks at a time and when someone is talking everyone else listens
- Raise your hand if you wish to say something
- Ride your bike when the instructor asks you to
- Follow instructions

Keep these simple and brief and coin them in positive language which will set the tone for the course. Many young people will have been told not to do this or that in many other circumstances so it may be refreshing to for them to be exposed only to positive language on a cycling course. Once the rules have been agreed you must enforce any infringement from the outset – when you will most likely be tested by the group. Remember that if you suggest a sanction you must follow that through or you will lose the respect of the group. So if you tell Davide that the next time he touches Kelly's bike he will be sent back to class and he does this again,

SEN

Cycling is for everyone and training can increase a person's enjoyment! Young people with Special Educational Needs (SEN) can be included in training and can progress at their own speed since the training is outcome based. Here are some tips for including people with SEN in training:
1. Give simple clear instructions
2. Apply same rules to all trainees
3. Use positive language (Do instead of Don't)
4. Praise or dismiss specific actions not the person
5. Change activities frequently
6. Plan sessions and be consistent

(See www.bikeability. dft.gov.uk for Delivering Inclusive Cycle Training module)

send him back to class. (Your co-instructor should accompany him back to class or to the school office explaining why he has been excluded).

Managing groups off road

While teaching Level 1 you will often be running the session in a school playground. Use the space well, utilising any playground markings to help with activities. Minimise distractions to trainees. Ensure that trainees have their back to the sun. Since you will be facing the sun, wear a peaked cap to protect your eyes rather than sunglasses which limits eye contact. Trainees should also have their backs to other distractions such as other pupils playing football. When not riding, bikes should be neatly stacked or left on the ground (with the chain facing upwards to avoid damage to it) so they won't fiddle with the bike and lose concentration while you are talking to them. They should step away from a bike on the ground which is a trip hazard. They should be riding most of the time rather than listening to theory so keep your talking to a minimum and set up riding activities and games quickly. Once you and your co-instructor have agreed that they have achieved the outcome move swiftly to the next activity.

Managing groups on road

Trainees must be able to stand where they can hear you and see what you are talking about. It is often a good idea to allow trainees to stand on the road where they can see better. You and your co-instructor can manage this so they are not obstructing traffic, moving them on and off the road as required. Getting trainees standing on the road can be useful in 'demystifying' the road space before they ride on the road. Many young people will have been taught to fear stepping on the road so showing them that roads are not scary if managed properly is a good transition activity. Seeing you communicate with drivers, watching drivers slow while passing someone standing in the road will help trainees appreciate the importance of communication, and also that drivers are people who do not wish to harm anyone.

There are potentially more distractions on road than in the more controllable off road environment. Be prepared to relocate if necessary such as when noise (from drilling or tree pruning for example) makes it hard for trainees to hear. If a passerby shows interest be polite. Your co-instructor could give them a flyer with contact details so they can find more information about training. Handing out a flyer is a good way to avoid having to explain what is happening at the expense of the trainee's learning time.

When demonstrating ensure that trainees are positioned in a place where they can see the whole demonstration

When teaching about how people behave on road use real events, such as drivers creeping out of side roads, as they occur. When demonstrating ensure that trainees are positioned in a place where they can see the whole demonstration. Ask questions while they are observing the demonstration so they are more engaged.

When it is time for your group to ride on the road you need to ensure that there are not too many trainees hanging around queueing while waiting to ride. Two or three can be waiting while the others observe, answer questions and offer peers feedback. Keeping trainees moving will keep them engaged and less likely to misbehave due to boredom. They will also be constantly learning!

Troubleshooting

Despite your best efforts you may, on occasion, have to deal with some difficult behaviour from your trainees or other people. Here are some situations that may arise and suggestions on how to deal with them:

Dominant trainee shouting out	Start with a quiet word from the co-instructor reminding the trainee of the ground rules. Avoid continually telling this person to be quiet or saying shush since they may be seeking attention using bad behaviour. Praise good behaviour ("Well done for putting your hand up"). If the person continues to shout out use peer pressure, suggesting you will all have to go back to school if this continues. If it does continue you must follow through your threat. Giving a dominant trainee some additional responsibility such as asking them go first and demonstrate may help them receive positive attention and so minimise their need to misbehave.
Distracted trainees not listening/ looking	Why are they distracted? If there is a distraction in the environment move your trainees. Consider changing the activity. Perhaps they have listened to you for too long! Show them a demonstration or get them riding. Use ground rules if required.
Quiet trainee not participating	A trainee may not be forthcoming with answers for many reasons. They may not know the answer, may be shy or not understand the question. You could reword the question and ask them directly. Note that this may put undue pressure on them so do be sensitive. Some people can learn well and get good outcomes even if they don't seem to be taking part. If a trainee refuses to participate in the practical activity it could be that they are scared and don't feel confident. You can't force them. They may need more off road training to feel better about their bike control. Have a chat with their teacher or parent after the session.

Disagreement with what you are teaching	This is unlikely with young people. Some adults may disagree with elements of the training such as riding in primary position ("in the way of drivers"). Discuss the logic of what you are teaching using risk assessment as a tool to analyse different positions. Use advice in The Highway Code if relevant. Also state that you are teaching a nationally agreed syllabus. There is no point in a protracted argument. If they remain unconvinced or refuse to ride in the manner you are teaching you can refuse to teach them. (There will be a clause to this effect in the consent form.)
Trainee makes no progress	Have you covered all the learning preferences? Do you know if they have any special educational needs? You cannot move through the syllabus with them so they may need some training outside the group. You must prioritise the rest of the group so you may need to make an arrangement for that trainee to have some 1 to 1 training or join another group.
Risky behaviour like riding with 'no hands'	Stop any risky riding immediately and explain what the hazards are. Use the ground rules and follow through any sanctions that you have threatened.
Extreme misbehaviour from trainee(s)	This could be trainees fighting, riding off, damaging property etc. If you have used some of the methods described above and still have no control over your group end the session, get back to base and discuss this with teachers or parents. Only if anyone is at imminent risk from such behaviour would it be acceptable to restrain a trainee. Call the school for help or even the police if necessary.
Interference from others (when to call the police)	Generally members of the public appreciate the fact that young people undergo training. If a driver or any other member of the public acts in an aggressive or threatening manner towards you or your group stop any activity where there is an imminent risk of harm. Note the driver's registration number and car make to report them to the police. Avoid engaging with them or responding to any taunts. Report any such incident or near miss. Call the police if you feel at all threatened. You will need to reassure trainees that such behaviour is very rare.

6.3 Outcomes, sub-outcomes and on-going assessment

Trainees progress as they achieve the riding outcomes. Your role is to:

- continually assess them
- tweak how they ride with feedback from you or from other trainees
- show them again
- get them to observe their friends,
- give them another go until they consistently ride correctly
- only then can you move through the syllabus to the next outcome

In order for you to assess them you need to know exactly what to watch out for. You need to observe the detailed outcomes or sub-outcomes. For example: in order for you to observe them achieve the outcome 'Able to stop quickly in an emergency' you will need to observe them:

- using 2 brakes
- bracing both arms
- shifting weight back on the saddle
- pushing back with their pedals - this is an additonal outcome. An extra achievement to enable you to differentiate and give able trainees an extra target.

You will need to know these detailed sub-outcomes in order to feedback to them and tweak their riding. There is little value just asking them to repeat something without adding value between each go. You will be clear what outcomes and sub-outcomes you are expecting to observe as well as any extension activity from your lesson plan (See Chapter 7).

Your role is to continually assess them, tweaking how they ride with feedback from you or from other trainees

6.4 **Structuring time**

Just as the course has a clear structure, a beginning, middle and end, so does each session and each activity you plan to teach during the session. (See graphic). Being aware of this structure will help you keep track of where you are within the course and should ensure that your teaching is pacey. You will be aware if you start waffling. Letting your trainees know the course, session and activity structure will help them feel more secure, and give them (and you) a sense of progress and achievement. In order to ensure you have a clear structure you will need to plan each session and each activity. See Chapter 7 for samples of structured lesson plans for each activity.

Course (8 Hours)	Session (2 Hours)	Activity (20 mins)
Week 1	Introduction	Theory/Demo
Week 2	Riding activity 1	Riding Practice
Week 3	Riding activity 2	Feedback
Week 4	Feedback	Riding Outcomes

Circle riding

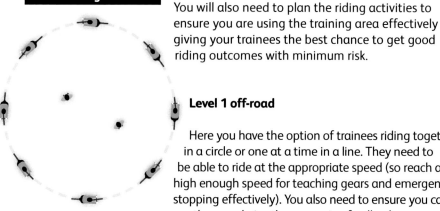

6.5 Running riding activities

You will also need to plan the riding activities to ensure you are using the training area effectively giving your trainees the best chance to get good riding outcomes with minimum risk.

Level 1 off-road

Here you have the option of trainees riding together in a circle or one at a time in a line. They need to be able to ride at the appropriate speed (so reach a high enough speed for teaching gears and emergency stopping effectively). You also need to ensure you can see them and give them ongoing feedback.

Linear riding

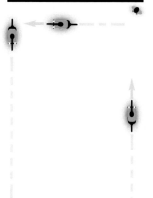

Circle riding is good for quick repeated practise such as starting & stopping and gears. Trainees can be controlled by an instructor riding with them setting the pace and space while the other instructor stands in the middle of the circle observing and giving instructions. This will also prepare the group for snaking on road.

You need to agree some rules for circle riding:

1. Leave enough room to stop between you and the person in front, about a bike's length
2. Stop if the person in front stops, slow down if they slow down and remain behind them (no overtaking)
3. Listen and follow any instructions

Linear riding is less risky and better for emergency stopping, looking back and signalling. Instructors can coach trainees giving individual feedback (See Chapter 9). Trainees can watch each other riding and give tips to their friends.

Level 2 (and 3) on-road

(Section 5.4 covers the risk management element of on road location choice)

When finding a location and setting up a riding activity on road you need to think about:

Are the trainees clear about the route they are expected to ride?
Ensure that all trainees observe an instructor demonstrating the exact route the trainees will be riding including where to start, stop and where to go after they have ridden.

Can the instructor(s) see everything?
Instructors must position themselves where they can see the trainee riding, the trainees waiting, and each other. They need to see in order to assess whether the trainee has achieved the outcome as well as to ensure their riding is not risky.

Are instructors able to control potential hazards?
Ensure an instructor is standing where they can stop the trainee if necessary (such as near the junction) - so they are positioned at the place of highest risk.

Can an instructor give instant feedback when the trainee ends their ride?
It is often a good idea for an instructor to be at the place where the trainee ends their ride to give feedback.

Where are the rest of the group standing?
Trainees should be able to watch each other ride and even offer feedback to their friends. They need to stand in a place where they can see and be seen by instructors.

Buddying

On most occasions your trainees will ride by themselves. There may be occasions where you decide to ride with them initially to help build their confidence. This may be for a particularly nervous trainee who may need some reassurance. You may decide to buddy someone if the location is busy or particularly complex. Your decision to ride with a trainee may be based on your risk assessment of the situation or as an educational tool so you can coach them on the move.

When using this technique, initially, ride slightly to their right, where you can communicate with them (though you may be blocking their view when they look behind). If you decide to ride with them a second time use your positioning, moving directly behind them or even to their left, to give them more independence. You will of course need to observe them riding independently in order for them to have achieved the outcome.

Planning

Now that you have a good grasp of how people learn you will have realised the importance of being prepared by planning activities, sessions and courses. In the next chapter you will find sample lesson plans for each riding activity in the National Standard.

7.
Lesson Plans

In this section we offer sample lesson plans for group training which you should find useful as you start teaching. You will need to adapt these to suit your trainees, the training environment and your trainees' aims.

7.1
Level 1 Lesson Plans

Level 1 should be completed during a 2 hour session for a group, each part taking around 10-15 minutes. (Although this will vary depending on the size and skills of the group). All Level 1 activities will take place on a playground large enough for the group to ride together in a circle and long enough for them to ride fast enough to need to change gear.

Many of these activities can be learnt while playing games. Keep your talking to a minimum, instead ask questions and use demonstrations. Most of the time they should be riding. In the lesson plans we suggest variations and additional activities which will enable you to challenge trainees to get outcomes more quickly and ensure that they are not bored while others in the group get more practice.

As mentioned in the previous chapter ensure you have learnt their names and agreed ground rules at the start of the course. At the start of each session link to the previous session, tell them the aim of the day and remind them of the ground rules.

Note that the lesson plans describe what trainees are doing. You will be able to extrapolate from that what you and your co-instructor are expected to do. So where the plan states 'Trainees suggest what is good to wear on a bike', you clearly will ask a question such as, "How would you dress for cycling?"

Outcome 1.1 - 1.2 **Clothing, equipment and bike checks**

Theory and observations	Trainees suggest what to wear on a bike. They see how you are dressed. They tie shoelaces and tuck in baggy trousers. They check that their clothing is appropriate for the weather. They watch you demonstrate how to adjust and fit a helmet and fit their own if they are wearing one.

Trainees suggest what they would check on a bike and how. They observe you or another trainee checking for:
- correctly inflated tyres (A)
- effective front and rear brakes (B)
- correct function of chain (C)
- handlebar stem secured to steerer tube (D)

They learn the 'ABCD'check: A (air) B (brakes) C (chain) D (direction)

Sample questions	• What would you check on a bike? • What parts of your bike can you adjust to fit you?
Additional learning points (optional)	How to clean and oil a chain. Existence and purpose of insertion limit marks on seat-post and stem. Use of quick-release or simple tools to adjust saddle height. Use of pump to inflate tyres to correct pressure.

Practical   Bikes may already have been assessed by instructors prior to arrival of trainees. Consider leaving some of the faults unfixed so that trainees may discover them. Trainees check their own/each other's bikes after learning each check, or after learning all 4 checks. Any faults discovered can be shown to the whole group. (At the start of subsequent sessions, trainees are asked to carry out their own checks under supervision).

    Regarding fitting, trainees observe you sitting on a small bike and suggest what adjustments can be made. They learn how to assess correct bike size, saddle height, and brake lever position.

Variations   More detailed checks (such as the M-check) are possible if appropriate for the trainee(s) level of understanding and there is time available.

Managing risk

What could happen	Action to prevent
Riders may be unused to recently raised saddles, and may initially have poor control.	Start with simple exercises, and keep adequate spacing between riders
Trainee is injured by mis-use of an Allen key or spanner while adjusting their bike	Teach trainees how to use a spanner/Allen key and supervise them

Outcome 1.3-1.7 **Starting, stopping and riding along**

Theory and observations

Trainees observe an instructor demonstrating poor techniques such as getting on without applying brakes so the bike isn't stable, scooting off rather than pedalling, riding while looking down and stopping with feet rather than brakes. They tell the instructor how to do it better by holding the brakes while mounting, setting the pedal, riding with brakes covered, looking ahead and stopping with brakes then putting a foot down.
They then observe an perfect demonstration.

Sample questions

- How can you stop the bike from moving when you want to get on and off?
- Which side of the bike do you get on?
- How can you make it easier to get on the bike?
- Where should your pedal be to push off smoothly?
- Where are your fingers as you ride along? Why?
- Where should you be looking?
- How many brakes do you use to stop?
- Where should your feet be all the time the bike is moving?

Additional learning points

They learn that if you lean the bike towards you it is easier to get on. They may need to push back as they come to a stoop to remain on the saddle. Some will be able to freewheel to a stop while their foot is in the starting position ready to go again.

Practical

Once you have recapped with checking questions they are ready to ride.
The trainees stand in a line with enough space between them to prevent the domino effect if one falls. They get on and off the bike. Once they do this well they can remain on a bike and get the pedal set ready to go. Agree the circle riding rules (see part 6.5) Consider using an instructor to set the pace and describe the riding circle. Each trainee sets off one behind the other. They slow down and stop on your count of '3,2,1 stop'. Many will be able to stop with their pedal ready to go again.

Variations The game 'Traffic lights' can make riding in a circle more fun. The game 'Stop in the box' may help trainees struggling to keep their feet on the pedal as they stop. Not all will be able to stop with their pedal set. So long as they can set their pedal swiftly ready to go again they have achieved the outcome.

Managing risk

What could happen	Action to prevent
Someone can't ride at all and tries to join in	Ask about experience before they get on the bikes. If you suspect there may be a non rider get them to ride separately or two at a time along a straight line and monitor their ability. Another instructor can work with a beginner while you work with the rest of the group.
They could crash into each other while riding in a circle	Define the route clearly and if there is any doubt have them follow an instructor. Ensure they are keeping to the circle riding rules.
Trainees ride too fast	Use instructor to control speed. Remind them of the no overtaking rule.

Outcome 1.8 **Use gears (where cycle has gears)**

Theory and observations

Trainees suggest why they have gears and show where their gears are, the names of parts and how to change them. They explain that they use low gear (low number) when riding slowly such as when starting off or climbing a hill, and higher gears when speeding up.

They observe the chain moving smoothly from sprocket to sprocket while changing gears one at a time. They observe that this only happens (on a bike with a derailleur) when the pedals are moving. They look at different shifting mechanisms and discover how to shift gears on their bike. They learn about having a steady cadence so their legs move at around the same speed whatever speed the bike is moving.

Two trainees have a short race, one is in the highest gear and the other in the lowest. They note that the person in the high gear struggles to start and is wobbly.

Sample questions

- Where are the gears on your bike?
- How many do you have?
- What are they for?
- Which gear is best for starting off?(Avoid specific numbers, rather use high/low)
- When should you change to a low gear so you start in a low gear?

Additional learning points

- They observe a bike with hub gears where they can shift without pedalling.
- They observe bikes with one gear such as a BMX/single speed bike.
- They learn to avoid using 'maximum crossover' gears (if derailleur system).

Practical   Once the points are recapped trainees practise using a circular riding activity, clockwise so that trainees' gears are visible to the instructor in the centre. One instructor leading to define the speed of the group. Trainees stop in their highest gear to feel how hard it is to start. They then vary their speed, start off and come to a stop shifting gear appropriately.

Repeat the exercise until group are changing to a low gear before stopping and higher gears when riding faster.

Variations   Utilise any available gradients in the training environment. The game traffic lights works well with this activity. With a pair or individual trainee, it can be useful to ride around a quiet park to give experience of different speeds/gradients. Keep this simple as it is easy to over complicate this topic.

Managing risk

What could happen	Action to prevent
Trainees may focus on gear shifters rather than where they are going and crash.	Keep plenty of space between trainees. Remind them to look up, and cover brakes.
When stopping, trainees shift down without pedalling. Chain jumps under load as they start again, causing a fall.	Watch for 'non-pedallers' as they slow down, prompting them if necessary. If you spot this move the shifters or spin the pedals before they ride again.

Outcome 1.9 Stop quickly with control (emergency stopping)

Theory and observations

Trainees consider when they may need to do an emergency stop.

They observe an instructor doing an emergency stop side-on so they can see their body shape and their weight shifting back. They observe that the instructor is covering and using both brakes, bracing their arms, staying in the saddle perhaps shifting back and keeping feet on pedals until the bike has stopped.

They observe this again while answering checking questions. Consider helping them remember by using '3 B's Both brakes, Brace arms, Bum back'.

Sample questions

- What could you do if a dog runs in front of you?
- What happens if you brake suddenly with the front/rear brake?
- How can you stop the back wheel lifting up?
- When should you put your feet on the ground?

Additional learning points

They could observe how each brake works noting that the rear wheel comes off the ground if the front or both brakes are squeezed suddenly and that the rear wheel skids yet the bike doesn't stop if just the rear brake is applied. Trainees can also learn that pumping the brakes can correct a skid. Some can demonstrate that using their feet to push back on the pedals helps shift weight back. They can suggest that stopping distance increases in wet weather.

Practical   This is a linear activity. Half the group line up in one corner of the playground opposite one instructor standing at the other end of the playground while the rest are opposite the other instructor (see diagram on page 101). They ride slowly towards an instructor and stop when the instructor asks them to. They should stop next to the instructor who can catch them if they get it wrong. They can also get brief feedback before riding to queue up with the other group to ride towards the 2nd instructor. Increase speed as their technique improves. (Once a trainee gets good outcomes you could ask them to stand with you to feedback to their friends).

Variations   Make it even more fun by adding small challenges, such as "How many seconds can you keep your feet on the pedals for after you've stopped?", and ask them to beat their personal best.
     Note different types of bike such as fixed gear and back pedal bikes.

Managing risk

What could happen	Action to prevent
Poor technique leads to rider going over handlebars	Start slowly increasing speed as technique improves. Ensure they stop near the instructor who can catch them.
Trainee's back wheel skids causes them to crash	Ensure the surface is appropriate and not loose, wet or slippery.
Trainee misbehave while waiting for their go	Keep it moving and feedback brief. Ask a trainee who messes around to stand with you to give feedback to their friends.

Outcome 1.10 **Swerve to avoid objects**

Theory and observations

Trainees consider when it would be appropriate to stop and when to swerve around a hazard such as a pothole or piece of glass. They also learn that it is better to swerve close to a hazard especially on road where they could bump into the kerb or a vehicle passing. (They may conclude that it is good to know what is behind at all times which links to the next activity).

They observe an instructor swerving around an object such as a water bottle. They see the instructor doing this heading towards them so they can see how close she is to the hazard. They also understand the importance of getting back to their original line after the swerve. Trainees will have been encouraged to cover their brakes throughout the Level 1 session however for this activity they must ensure they don't pull their brakes while swerving.

Sample questions

• What would you do if you came across a pothole/piece of glass in your path?
• Would it be better to swerve wide or close to the object?
• What line do you want to take after the swerve?

Additional learning points

With adults, consider showing them the technique of flicking the front wheel towards the object then away which enable a faster tighter swerve (it's a bit making an S-shape wiggling around the hazard).

Practical

This is another linear activity where trainees get to either swerve around a water bottle or around an instructor standing in the middle of playground. Trainees continue riding after swerving getting back to their original line as quickly as possible. Encourage them to increase speed as they get more confident.

Variations   Use cone spanners to create a gate. (See image below). Narrow the gap between the spanners to make this more challenging.

Trainees may be interested to look at additional emergency techniques such as bunny hopping over curbs or riding over lines (such as tram tracks) ensuring their front wheel approaches these at 90° angle. This could be included if time allows since they are not National Standard outcomes.

Managing risk

What could happen	Action to prevent
Trainees ride over the object and skid	Some objects such as flat cones may cause the wheel to skid if they ride over it so use bottles with water in, which will generally just fall over if hit.
Trainees brake while swerving and crash	Start slowly to build confidence and check technique. Ensure you remind them to stay off the brakes.

Outcome 1.11 Looking all around including behind

Theory and observations

This activity begins to plant ideas that will be relevant when they go on road. Trainees will start thinking about core concepts such as communication and making eye contact.

Trainees observe an instructor riding away from them glancing and staring back at them. Trainees understand that it is important to look back not only to know what is there but also to ensure that they have been seen. They need to be able to look back over each shoulder and take in information while continuing to ride in a straight line. They learn that touching their chin to a shoulder will give them a better view as will dropping their hand which enables them twist their waist for an even better view.

Sample questions

• Why do you need to look back on a bike?
• How long should you look back for? (Long enough to get the information and communicate but not too long so you still know what is in front).

Additional learning points

They need to gather information about people behind such as their speed and distance. The left shoulder check is often to look out for other cyclists. Pedalling while looking will help with balance.

Practical

This is another linear activity with the 2 instructors at opposite corners of the playground with a group of trainees who will ride, one at a time, away from the instructor and look back over one shoulder and call out how many fingers instructor is holding up. They should also be encouraged to make eye contact with the instructor where possible. They could practise looking right then turning right to join the other instructor and her group then reverse this doing only left shoulder looks. This will help reinforce a link between looking and turning in the same direction.

Variations

Challenge trainees to look back longer and drop a hand to see further around. Instructors can ride behind trainees especially when teaching individuals and vary their position making it harder to see. Try a group ride, one person behind the other, asking them to check back to find out the colour of the bike/jumper/gloves etc. of the person behind.

Managing risk

What could happen	Action to prevent
Trainee wobbles and falls	Build up skills by getting them to make quick glances. Ensure they keep pedalling and ride at a fast enough to aid balance.
Trainee changes direction and crashes into fence or other trainees	Manage the logistics of this to anticipate that while practicing trainees may change direction. Don't do this close to potential hazards. Ensure trainees are clear where they go after their turn.
Trainees misbehave while waiting for their go	Keep trainees moving and your feedback brief.

Outcome 1.12 **Signalling right and left without loss of control**

Theory and observations

Trainees suggest why a rider may need to offer a hand signal and to whom. Off their bike, they demonstrate a signal by holding their arm out straight at ninety degrees from their body with the palm of the hand held flat in a vertical position. They say why it is important to always check behind prior to signalling.

They observe an instructor (check back) signal (check again) and turn and explain why the instructor's hands were back on the handlebars before turning. They also explain why the instructor checked back again just before the turn.

Sample questions

- How do cyclists tell other road users that they intend to turn?
- Who needs to know that you are about to turn?
- Do you have more control of your bike steering with one hand or two?

Additional learning points

Trainees consider how long to signal for to ensure that other road users see the signal - this will increase in line with the volume of traffic. A signal is not needed if there are no people to signal to.

Practical

Trainees could practise a signal one at a time with checking back - just to ensure they can ride one handed, or they could be asked to look before signalling from the outset as it is such a good instinct to instil. Riders cycle away from the instructor in a straight line and are asked to signal either left or right. Those that aren't yet confident enough to ride one handed can be asked to lift up their hands briefly and then extend the time and distance from the handlebars until they can signal.

Trainees will then practise the turning sequence combining a glance back, a signal, hands back on bars, a final check, then a turn - doing this for both a left and right turn.

Variations   The 'Mirror Game' where trainees copy the gestures of an instructor they are riding towards can help people learn quickly. Skilled riders who are confident signalling can be asked to slow down while signalling using only one brake or challenged to signal for a longer time. For an individual this can be practised with the instructor cycling behind the trainee.
Skilled trainees can practise looking back, signalling and slowing down all at the same time.

Managing risk

What could happen	Action to prevent
Rider wobbles and falls off	Ensure riders are confident in lifting each hand away from handlebars before attempting to signal.
Rider wobbles	Discourage riders from gripping their handlebars too tightly or leaning too heavily on their handlebars.
Rider wobbles	Encourage the rider to keep pedalling, being in a comfortable gear will help with control.

Outcome 1.13 Share space off road with pedestrians and other cyclists

Observable outcomes

Trainees describe how they would like people to ride around them if they are walking in a park or on a canal towpath. They suggest that cyclists should ride at an appropriate speed not much faster than a walking pace. Riders need to wait patiently behind pedestrians or slower riders. They should say 'excuse me' or politely ting a bell to indicate that they wish to pass and when passing they should pass wide and generally to the right.

Sample questions

- How would you like cyclists to behave near you if you were walking in the park?
- Would you prefer someone behind you to ring a bell, say 'excuse me' or wait?

Additional learning points (optional)

- Discuss whether or not it is appropriate to ting the bell.
- Discussion of whether it is better to use the roads rather than shared space such as canal tow paths where cycling may be deemed anti-social.

Practical

Three trainees to start to walk in a line down the playground, when they are about a third of the way ask three riders to ride behind them and decide if and how to get by. Trainees do a similar activity with three people riding slowly while 3 others either overtake or decide to remain behind. Play the game 'Dozy pedestrian' where the rider rides behind you ready to slow or stop as you move across their path.

Variations

If the school teachers agree, consider asking the riders to cycle across the playground during playtime. Ride around the path in a park with an individual trainee discussing whether or not it is appropriate to pass walkers.

Managing risk

What could happen	Action to prevent
Trainees collide with walker/slow rider	Ensure they are clear that there is an option to wait patiently so there is no need to always try and pass. Ensure this whole activity is done at low speeds.
Trainees collide while turning in the playground	Agree that all trainees turn in the same direction when they reach the end of the playground. If they do not cycle in the same direction stop the drill.

Riders need to wait patiently behind pedestrians or slower riders

They should say 'excuse me' or politely ting a bell to indicate that they wish to pass and when passing they should pass wide and generally to the right

7.2

Level 2 Lesson Plans

Level 2 should be completed in 6 to 8 hours, depending on the size and skill level of the group. It should be delivered in 1.5 to 2 hour sessions. The lesson should cover at least 2 riding activities in a 2 hour session , including a ride of a reasonable distance from base and between locations. The locations are on roads with traffic and should get progressively busier as trainees work through Level 2. The core skills they are learning are how to interact with people in cars so the more opportunity they have to ride with drivers the better the learning outcomes. If you find that a location is very quiet consider relocating.

All Level 1 outcomes have been achieved. Set up each session reminding trainees of ground rules and the aims of the session and course, linking to the previous session. Ensure they have checked their bikes under your supervision. Consider a brief warm up snaking practice in the play-ground before heading out. Ride to locations away from the school, where they can stack their bikes and not obstruct or disturb people.

Gather the group around so they can see you and understand what they are learning at a particular drill site. Keep your talking to a minimum and focus on trainee involvement through questioning and demonstrations. After 5-10 minutes of theory trainees should be riding. Don't worry if you haven't covered all the learning points since you can add points during the drill as they are riding.

Keep the students involved whether they are riding, or observing and offering feedback to their friends. There should be no more than two trainees at a time waiting to have a go by the roadside. The rest are

standing with you, your co-instructor or positioned where they can see. Ensure that they understand what to change between each go so they get outcomes quickly and move on. While it is good to check that they are putting into practice what they have learnt while moving as a group between locations this isn't crucial. Outcomes are only achieved when a trainee rides independently.

When you observe the outcomes from the group either move to the next activity or, if there is time, repeat the same activity at a more challenging location.

Remember these principles while teaching Level 2:

- Less teacher talking more trainee answering, watching and riding
- Trainees are in sight of at least 1 instructor at all times
- You have plan B locations and more challenging options
- Trainees are in the best position to observe demonstrations
- Strategic bike stacking will ensure that the stronger trainees go first, this can be varied letting other go first later in the course
- Trainees ride one at a time
- While waiting they should be involved and giving feedback to their friends
- Keep up the pace and move on once they get the outcome

Outcome 2.1-2.6 Beginning and ending an on-road journey, looking around and signalling and passing parked cars

Theory and observations

Trainees observe that the best place to set off from is where they can best see and be seen yet not where they obstruct other road users. They learn that people already moving go first so they need to check back and only go when clear. Trainees observe how far a car door opens and where to ride in the road. They learn about the importance of looking back to ensure drivers behind see them. They understand that they have equal right of way to a driver coming towards them and learn to hold their line and negotiate with eye contact to encourage the driver to slow so they can pass each other. They discuss when and whether to signal before pulling in. They observe an instructor starting and ending a journey showing them the route they will be riding.

Sample questions

- Where would you get on the bike to start your journey? (Give 3 options)
- How do you ensure drivers behind notice you? (Glance back)

Additional learning points (optional)

They learn that where they can match the speed of the moving traffic they should ride in the traffic stream, the primary position. They should also ride in this position when they need to such as when riding away from parked cars. When they don't need to ride in the primary position, they can use the secondary position, to the left of the traffic stream. They learn to pull in by the kerb and walk, not ride, on the pavement. Trainees could consider acknowledging with a wave or smile any driver behind them.

Practical   One instructor is positioned up the road and waits to receive trainees. The other stands either with the trainee about to ride or on the road/pavement opposite them with the rest of the group. Two trainees wait their turn. Each waits for a signal from the instructor then decides when to go. The rest of the group can wait in a position where they can observe and give feedback. Once trainees have pulled in they wait and observe with the receiving instructor. They give feedback to their friends then walk back on the pavement to go again until they get the outcomes.

Variations   Extend the run to include a large gap between parked cars. You could cross trainees over the road and ask them to ride back. Extend this run to incorporate passing side roads (see next section). Once they have got the basics move to a busier location to repeat the activity. Discuss what they would do where there are no parked cars (or relocate to such a place).

Managing risk

What could happen	Action to prevent
Trainee loses control and crashes; or moves left when a driver is behind due to nerves	While they may have demonstrated excellent L1 skills in the playground some young people take a while to adapt to road conditions. Consider buddy riding with a nervous trainee. Let them go last so they see their friends riding successfully.
Trainees misbehave and get distracted while waiting to have a turn	Avoid having more than 2 trainees waiting to ride and involve others to watch their friends and offer constructive feedback..

Outcome 2.7 Pass side roads and crossroads riding along the major road

Theory and observations	Trainees learn the rules at a give way line (or a stop line). They understand that they have right of way when riding along the main road – they 'go first'. They also learn that drivers often need to creep out so may edge over the give way line and their car bonnet may extend into the major road. Trainees have a look by standing on the give way line to see why drivers creep out. This works best if the junction has parked cars on the major road. Trainees realise that they need to ride wide of any junction in order to get seen by drivers early. They glance back on approach to the junction and look into the side-road to the left (and to the right at a crossroad). They also check ahead for drivers wishing to turn into the minor road. (See diagram p135).
Sample questions	• Who goes first, people on the major road or the minor road? • Why? (Because people on the major road are moving in a straight line) • What may a driver think if you slowed down or moved left approaching a side road? (that you are turning left)
Additional learning points (optional)	They learn that keeping pedalling and maintaining speed helps drivers realise that they're not planning to turn into the side-road. They understand that they may need to move further to the right to prevent drivers passing at junctions in some circumstances.

Practical   One instructor monitors the junction and one receives the trainee and gives feedback. Where the training is at a significantly busier location than the first activity (2.1-2.6), one instructor could monitor their starting off. Two trainees walk to the start point while the remainder wait with the instructor who is monitoring the junction to observe their friends and give feedback. Once trainees have completed their run they wait with the receiving instructor to help with feedback. They walk back along the pavement and cross the side road (supervised by an instructor) to walk back to the starting point.

Variations   Try this on roads of different width to assess trainees understanding of how their position influences drivers behind. You could time when they set off to ensure that there is a driver behind to give them the experience of managing that situation. Repeat activity at a crossroad.

Managing risk

What could happen	Action to prevent
Trainee gets frightened when there is a driver in the side road and stops giving up on their right of way	Ask them to pull over and watch other trainees perform the activity. Consider riding with them once to build their confidence coaching them as they ride. Recap the 'who goes first rule' and show them drivers slowing to check before pulling out onto the major road.
Trainee forgets earlier outcomes such as looking back before starting	This may happen if the new location is busier and they feel more nervous. Consider in such circumstances having an instructor at the start point.

Outcome 2.8 (Junction turns 1) Turn right into a major road, do a U-turn then left into a minor road

Theory and observations

Trainees understand that before any manoeuvre they must always check behind and decide if there is a need to signal. The group should discuss their road position at the mouth of a junction. Make certain that trainees understand that they can ensure drivers remain behind if they ride centrally in the lane. Trainees choose where they would wait for a right turn. Once they grasp the principle that one vehicle moves through a junction at a time they decide that they would remain behind a driver waiting at a junction. Just as drivers creep out of a side-road to see if it is clear to turn so can a rider move ahead of the give way line if they need to. They understand that if the major road is clear they can keep moving through the junction. In order to spend less time on the wrong side of the road they observe that a straight line then arcing right is preferable to cutting the corner. Trainees observe a demonstration of the right turn, a U-turn then the left turn into the side road. In the case of a U-turn, they understand that all other road users go first so this is only done when the road is clear in both directions.

They also observe that a rider may prevent a driver passing when turning left by looking back before the junction and turning into the side road positioned in the centre of the lane (where they can also see what is coming down the side road).

Sample questions

- Where would you position yourself at the junction to turn right? (Give 3 options a. Far left b. centre of lane and c. far right?
- Who goes first if you wish to do a u-turn? (Everyone else)
- How do you communicate that you're turning left? (Glance left and signal left if anyone needs to know)

Additional learning points

If a junction sweeps wide and the single lane becomes two (unmarked) lanes, riders take a central position in the right hand lane. In some circumstances taking the lane on the major road before turning left will ensure drivers don't overtake and pull left cutting up a rider.

Practical Two trainees walk to the start point on the minor road while the rest observe either opposite the junction or at the corner depending on sight lines. An instructor monitors the junction standing with the observing trainees asking them for comments and feedback about their friends riding. The other instructor monitors the U-turn asking trainees to stop if they look like they're deciding to turn inappropriately. The instructor at the junction can indicate the next person to start riding once the first trainee is coming to the end of their turn. The instructor at the junction can supervise all road crossings on foot.

Variations Each junction turn can be taught as a separate manoeuvre. This activity could be taught at a dog-leg (staggered) junction with an instructor positioned at each junction. The U-turn would then have to be taught elsewhere. Discuss who goes first at a crossroad with more advanced trainees.

Managing risk

What could happen	Action to prevent
Trainee doesn't check around properly prior to a U-turn	Until trainees demonstrate correct decision making and actions before a U-turn an instructor is able to stop the trainee turning in to someone who is there.
Trainee pulls out of junction without observing if there is a vehicle on the major road	The instructor at the junction will be positioned where they can instruct the trainee to look or to stop the trainee before they ride onto the major road.

Outcome 2.9 (Junction turns 2) Turn right into a minor road, do a U-turn then left into a major road

Theory and observations

By this point on the course trainees will have an understanding of the importance of looking back, deciding if and when to signal and road positioning to control other road users. Key to this manoeuvre is understanding the importance of beginning to look early in order to give themselves time to move right across the traffic stream. This should be taught on a fairly busy road. Walk with trainees along the major road asking them when they would start the checks behind and where on the main road they would wait to turn. They understand that oncoming drivers have priority and they only turn when clear. Once they understand how quickly things can change they will know why a final check back (lifesaver check) is especially necessary for this turn. After the U-turn on the minor road they observe a demonstration of an instructor turning left from a minor to a major road and are able to explain why the instructor is positioned centrally in the lane even when turning left. (See diagram p134).

Sample questions

- Who goes first when you wish to turn, you or oncoming drivers?
- What do you do just before turning right? (Check back again)

Additional learning points (optional)

Some major roads are wide enough to let drivers pass on the trainee's nearside while they are waiting to turn into the junction. Where the trainee is not sure if this is the case they should wait in the middle of the lane preventing drivers passing.

It is worth mentioning that if trainees aren't able to move right due to a constant stream of drivers they can always pull over to the left and walk across.

Practical	Two trainees wait at the start point on the major road while the rest of the group are opposite the junction with an instructor so they can observe and comment. The other instructor could be at the start point since this road may be quite busy. An instructor at the start could also manage to time the trainee's ride to ensure that there is a driver behind that they need to communicate with. Alternatively the other instructor could be at the U-turn point especially if they haven't yet got the U-turn outcome. Once trainees have pulled over to the left of the major road they should be instructed to walk to the junction to where an instructor can supervise their road crossing.
Variations	This can be taught as 2 separate turns or as one loop including a U-turn. It is possible to reverse the loop starting on the minor road and performing the U-turn on the main road.

Managing risk

What could happen	Action to prevent
Trainee misjudges speed of oncoming driver and turns	If you think an trainee may lack confidence or understanding of who goes first consider riding with them initially so you can ensure that they wait until it is clear to go.
Trainee is too scared to move right across the traffic stream	Use the buddy technique described above. Also ensure that they understand that they can always pull over to the left and wait for space or cross on foot.

Turn right into a major road, do a U-turn then left into a minor road

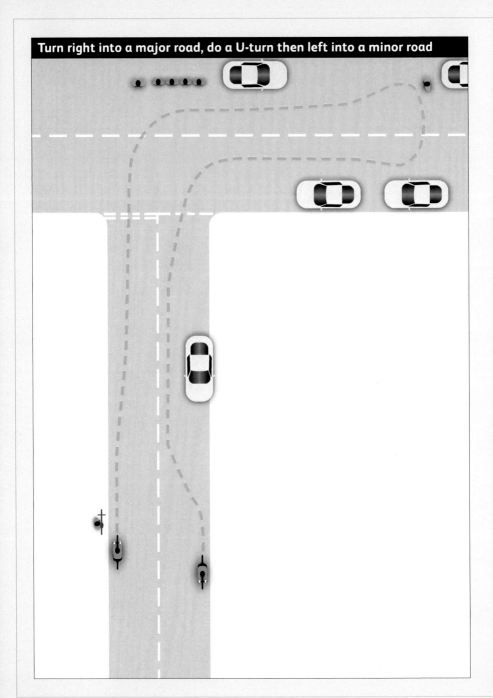

Turn right into a minor road, do a U-turn then left into a major road

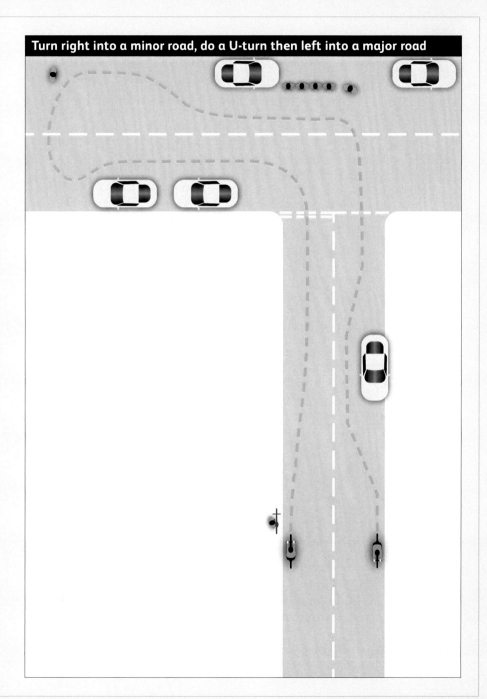

Outcome 2.10 **Explain decisions made and demonstrate an understanding of low risk riding strategy**

Outcome 2.11 **Demonstrate a basic understanding of The Highway Code including 'who goes first', relevant road signs and lines**

Theory and observations

Both these outcomes are observed throughout Level 2 training by trainees answering questions. Ensure that all trainees get the opportunity to answer a question about the importance of checking back and riding positioned where they are seen by drivers. All trainees should also have the opportunity to answer a question about priority in different circumstances. It is worth establishing a principle that people going straight generally have priority over people turning. Aim to teach at locations that have clear road markings and signs where possible and refer to these – checking that trainees understand what they indicate. Point out relevant road signs discussing clues about signs from their colour and shape.

Additional learning points (optional)

Throughout the course check trainees understanding of signs they encounter either while snaking to locations or at the activity sites.

Outcome 2.12 (Optional) Decide where on and off road cycle infrastructure can help a journey and demonstrate correct use

Theory and observations

Where there is specific cycle infrastructure such as cycle lanes, paths or shared paths with pedestrians, trainees decide if and how they would use such infrastructure. Trainees understand that there is no obligation for riders to use such infrastructure and that in some circumstances they may be more visible to drivers riding out of the cycle lanes, especially if the lane takes them too close to a junction or too near parked cars. Show trainees the sign indicating a shared path with pedestrians and discuss whether its better to use this or to remain on the road. (See 7.1.13 for using shared space with walkers).

Sample questions	• Do you have to use a cycle lane if there is one? (No, not if it puts you in a less visible position.)
Additional learning points (optional)	When using a cycle lane riding on the right of it may make the rider more visible and make drivers give more space when passing. Trainees understand that some drivers don't appreciate the space riders need and expect cyclists to use cycle lanes if they are provided so may hoot or get angry. Trainees understand how to respond in such situations and that it is often a good ideas to ignore an angry driver who hoots noting that at least the driver has seen them.
Practical	If time allows, in addition to discussing the topic near a cycle lane trainees could repeat an earlier activity such as passing a side road or passing parked cars where they decide whether or not to use a painted cycle lane.
Variations	If available, trainees observe some good cycle infrastructure such as a wide cyclists only contraflow, or a road with through access only to people on bikes and access only to residents on cars.

Managing risk

What could happen	Action to prevent
Trainee gets shouted at or beeped by a driver while riding on a road where a cycle lane is provided	(See above) Trainees discuss why this may happen in advance and how to respond in such circumstances. In extreme circumstances where a driver seriously abuses the rider whether by swearing or passing close to punish the rider note the drivers car details and report this as an incident.

Outcome 2.13 (Optional) Go straight ahead at crossroads (minor road to minor road)

Theory and observations

If trainees discuss this towards the end of Level 2 a couple of quick questions should demonstrate whether they understand the principles of positioning in the middle of the lane at junctions. They understand that anyone on the main road has priority including drivers turning from the main road into a side road. If a person is indicating to turn right from the opposite side road a person going straight should have priority. Not all drivers will remember this perhaps, so trainees need to ensure drivers turning have seen them by making eye contact before proceeding straight ahead.

Additional learning points (optional)

Mention here that sometimes drivers forget to signal so even though the driver emerging from the side road opposite isn't indicating to turn it is always worth making eye contact and looking for other hints as to the driver's intention such as looking at the angle of their car wheels.

Practical

Position an instructor at each junction. Two trainees walk to the start point and set off one at a time. The rest of the group remain at the corner to watch and offer feedback about their friends' ride.

Variations

Try this at a junction that sweeps out forming 2 lanes. The rider will remain in the middle of the left hand lane if going straight on.

Outcome 2.14 Use mini and single lane roundabouts

Where there are mini roundabouts near the school and you have time in the Level 2 course it is worth teaching this at Level 2. For detailed lesson plans for roundabouts see the next section covering Level 3 (7.3.2).

7.3

Level 3 Lesson Plans

Once trainees have demonstrated good Level 2 riding outcomes and an understanding of core principles of position and communication they are ready to apply these principles using more complex infrastructure and on roads where there are more drivers who may be driving at faster speeds.

On rare occasions you may move straight onto Level 3 with a strong group of primary school pupils on completion of Level 2. Be sure to remain within the maximum ratio for L3 of 2:6. It is more likely that you will be teaching Level 3 to secondary school pupils and to adult individuals. An adult who already rides may be able to complete Levels 2 and 3 within a 2 hour session. A group of two or three young people could complete Level 3 in 2 or 3 hours.

Level 3 lessons with individuals or pairs will be very dynamic with trainees both observing and being observed by you. Throughout the training you will be pulling over for quick chats and feedback. What you cover will depend on the location and needs of your trainees. The Level 3 environment will be on multi-lane A-roads, traffic lights controlled junctions, major roundabouts and gyratories and roads where the speed limit is 30mph or higher. Most of the infrastructure in Level 3 is described as 'optional' which allows for Level 3 completion even in places where there may be no specific infrastructure such as a roundabouts or bus lanes, but where a trainee's ability to demonstrate advanced road positioning and communication can still be observed.

You will generally be riding behind your trainee(s) through the Level 3 environment, pulling over to discuss points and the approach to different types of situation. In some instances you may decide to ask your trainee to ride behind you either to observe how you ride or to test their assertiveness with drivers behind (such as preventing a bus driver passing by their positioning and eye contact). Riding as a pair is a Level 3 outcome.

Some Level 3 outcomes will be covered through a conversation with your trainee, (even before you meet them) such as (3.1) Prepare for a journey when you will discuss weather gear, route planning, carrying stuff, locking bikes, lights and night riding etc. Demonstration of advanced hazard perception (3.4) is covered dynamically as you encounter situations such as dealing with a poor road surface or understanding where lorry driver blind spots are located.

In this section we provide lesson plans for learning about using multi-lane roads, including roads with bus lanes where cycling is allowed, roundabouts and traffic lights.

Outcome 3.2 **Advanced road positioning: Turn on and off multi-lane roads**

Outcome 3.6 **Manage vehicles that pull in and stop such as buses in bus lanes**

Outcome 3.8 **Ride on roads with speed above 30 mph**

Theory, observations and practical

Trainees will have a good grasp of the riding principles of communication and positioning. When at the location it is worth observing how other people use the road. Trainees discuss whether or not they need to ride in the traffic stream or to the left of it positioning may depend on factors such as the width of the road, the speed of the driver, the speed of the trainee, any traffic calming devices etc. Ride behind your trainee along the road encouraging them to check behind regularly. Initially, ride protectively a little to their right. As the trainee gains confidence, adjusting your position moving left so they take more responsibility. You could ask them to ride behind you for a while to observe you and to help them gain more confidence communicating back.

Ride in a bus lane agreeing a central position as the best place to ride. Note other riders may pass on their left, so glancing left is important. Your trainees should consider regulating their speed so slowing down if a bus has overtaken and wishes to pull in.

Avoid riding too close to any vehicle in front. Riding to the right of the vehicle will enable a trainee to overtake should the vehicle pull in, without swerving or altering their line significantly. To overtake a bus at a stop where it is picking up people, glance back and move right (even into the next lane) to overtake, riding wide of the bus so the driver will see them in the mirror. The trainee should allow a bus driver signalling to pull out of a bus stop to go first by slowing down.

In order to turn right off a multi-lane road the rider may need to push into a fast stream of traffic using eye contact and signalling, waiting for a gap or for a driver to let them in. Encourage the trainee to move to the middle of the nearside lane first then move to the middle of the next lane going a lane at a time.

It is worth buddying them the first time they do this so from behind them you could move first making a space for them to move in front of you. Once they have done this a couple of times ask them to ride behind you and do the same. This should empower them and build up their confidence.

Sample questions	• Where would you position yourself in a bus lane? (Centrally) • Where would you wait in a lane before turning right? (It depends on the width of the lane and whether or not I am happy to be passed by vehicles on both sides)
Additional learning points	A discussion about the speed of a traffic stream is relevant here. At speeds of 30mph or above it is harder to remain in the traffic stream and it is tempting to tuck close by the kerb. This is risky since there is no escape route when riding too near the kerb (as discussed in Level 2). All the same Level 2 principles apply - your trainee must demonstrate continued glancing back so they are aware of every driver that passes and adjust their position if they see a driver is too close. Discuss with them the effect of heavy high sided vehicles as they overtake.

Managing risk

What could happen	Action to prevent
A trainee is too scared to ride in a busy L3 environment and becomes upset	If training through Level 2 has been organic and your trainees have experienced busier roads as they progress there should not be too much difference between end of L2 and start of L3. You could revisit level 2 infrastructure to build up their confidence.
Trainee misjudges the speed of a vehicle behind and pulls right in front of the driver	Build up confidence gradually and buddy them so you are able to assess their judgement skills well in advance of their riding independently.

Outcome 3.2 Advanced road positioning: Roundabouts

Theory and observations

Trainees observe how people use a roundabout by standing where they have a good view near a roundabout. Ask them questions to ensure they understand priority, that the roundabout road is the main one-way road and people on it go first. People wishing to join it give way to the right. When riding on a roundabout mention that every exit they don't use can be treated like a side road they are passing – so they need to keep wide, ride centrally in a roundabout lane and make eye contact with anyone about to enter the roundabout. If there is more than one lane establish that generally they use the inner lane if turning right off a roundabout and remain in the left hand lane if turning left or going straight. (If they observe how drivers use a roundabout they will see this).

Discuss when to check back and signal. Trainees should conclude that on entering a roundabout they signal the direction they intend to leave (even though they will always turn left onto a roundabout). They should only signal left to leave the roundabout after the exit before their exit.

Sample question	• How many roads are there? (Number of roads plus the roundabout road)
Additional learning points (optional)	It is often a good idea to signal right if intending to remain on the roundabout to ensure drivers remain behind and don't cut up the rider. As a general principle when using major roundabouts and gyratory systems it is good to remain central in the appropriate lane even if this means slowing the traffic stream a little. This ensures the cyclist does not get squeezed.
Practical	Generally it is a good idea to ride with a trainee the first time. Ensure other trainees can see the technique. It is essential that you and your co-instructor can observe. Positioning of instructors could be at the entry and exit junctions or even in the middle of the roundabout if possible.
Variations	Start with mini-roundabouts (which are optional at Level 2)

Managing risk

What could happen	Action to prevent
You lose sight of your trainee due to the nature of the roundabout	If there isn't a position for you to observe and you are not with another instructor, ride with the trainees hanging back so they make their own decisions but you can observe them the whole time.

Outcome 3.3 Passing queuing traffic, knowing when and how to filter

Outcome 3.5 Using traffic light controlled junctions including those with advanced stop boxes

Theory and observations

Stand with your trainees and observe the lights sequence and how people behave in cars and on bikes. Remind them that only green means 'go'. Discuss the three options a rider has of hanging back, filtering either right or left of the stationary traffic and risk assess each option. Trainees should conclude that staying back in the traffic stream is the least risky option (apart from exposure to exhaust fumes) and that filtering right is often less risky than filtering left.

They should observe how drivers pull away from lights. That is, a gap opens between each vehicle which can be useful for the rider as it allows them to move back into the traffic stream if the lights change while they are filtering right. Demonstrate this so they see you doing this. You will need to time your demonstration to make this work.

If the junction has an Advanced Stop Box (ASB), show them that it is better to stop in front of the traffic in the middle of the traffic stream, central in the ASB. Where there is no ASB then to position themselves behind to the right of the first car in the queue will enable the rider to indicate to the driver that they plan to pull into the traffic stream when the lights change.

Discuss the hazards of filtering with the trainees. Eliciting responses in how to minimise these risks including: people stepping between stationary vehicles, motorcyclists filtering either from behind or in oncoming traffic, drivers pulling out of a junction through a gap to turn right, oncoming drivers, the drivers moving off, a driver deciding to U-turn out of the queue etc. Ensure that they understand that filtering should be slow riding. They should be on the lookout for gaps in the queue near junctions and that they should slow more when passing high sided vehicles in case a pedestrian is crossing.

Sample question	• What would you do if there was a queue of drivers as you approached a red light?)
Practical	Because the light sequence and start off of queuing drivers may vary it is a good idea to practice this activity by moving along a road with a number of lights so your trainee gets a chance to try different situations. Letting them ride behind to observe your behaviour can be quite enlightening particularly as the 'normal' behaviour of cyclists is to filter left and right filtering is perceived as riskier.

Managing risk

What could happen	Action to prevent
Your trainee goes through a light which changes leaving you waiting at the red light	Ensure your trainee habitually checks back after moving through lights so they should see you are not with them. Prepare them for this possibility telling them to pull over and wait if you are not there.

Outcome 3.7 Ride in pairs or in groups and with other cyclists

Theory, observations and practical

Riding with friends as a group can be fun and even more fun if you ride in a manner that will keep you all together. The principles covered in the section about moving trainees (Chapter 8) can be applied to riding with a friend or friends. Here are some guidelines for this:

- Agree how you plan to ride in advance including riding speed, the route and who leads so people's expectations are managed. It is not always necessary to stick to cycle lanes when group riding or even the quiet cycle routes since often a group can take up a whole lane on a major road.
- Consider exchanging mobile numbers in case someone gets lost.
- Suggest that stronger riders stay towards the back and the slower riders are near the front to set the pace. Encourage riders to check back ensuring the rest of the group are with them. If you lose sight of the rider(s) behind slow down or pull in to regroup. Shout out any issues to ensure riders in front slow or pull over.
- Avoid filtering through traffic, front riders stop behind drivers at lights and move through lights in the traffic stream.
- Consider politely preventing drivers from passing until there is room for them to clear the whole group. (Be sensible about this - most drivers will appreciate the communication and hang back, if a driver is clearly irate, get everyone to move left to let them pass).
- When turning at T-junctions It is often a good idea to 'request' drivers to give up on their right of way to keep the group together. This isn't necessary when there are just two of you.
- The rear riders move (right) before front riders when changing lane to claim the space and prevent anyone overtaking as the group move over.

Practical   While riding with your trainee you can demonstrate these principles by getting them to notice how you ride and when you move right or come up along side them. At Level 3 let them have a go riding behind you.

8.
Moving Trainees

Here we look at ways of moving your trainees on road to, from and between locations. We call moving trainees on road 'snaking'. We will also look at how to move pairs of riders and individuals.

You may, on occasion, need to walk with your group. We will explore when this is appropriate and look at techniques to ensure you move people efficiently and with minimum risk.

8.1 Snaking

Moving trainees on road on bikes means you can
be more dynamic, ride more, have more fun (than
walking bikes to the locations), and get further from
the base. The best way to move a group of riders
is in a line, one behind the other (or occasionally
doubled up in pairs). This is called snaking. In order
for a trainee to take part in a 'snake' they need to
have good bike control so they will need to have
finished Level 1. They do not however need any
understanding of road riding to take part in snaking.

It is possible to move up to 12 people with 2
instructors in a single line. 12:2 is the maximum ratio
for Level 2 training and means that the snake is quite
long. Using the 'doubling-up' technique becomes
more important the larger the group.

Doubling up

There are occasions where you may wish to make the snake shorter and
wider by getting the riders to ride in pairs. This is called 'doubling up' and
is useful when moving through lights or when you wish to stop anyone
overtaking. To do this the front instructor will shout 'double up!' and show 2
fingers to signal this. The second trainee moves to the right of the first, the
fourth to the right of the third and so on until the group is riding 2 abreast.
The first, third (etc) trainees should slow down while the 2nd and 4th (etc)
speed up. The reverse of this needs to happen to move back to single file
again. If you plan to use this technique, practise it first in the playground.

*The principle of snaking is that 2 instructors work as
a team to keep the group together, moving as one
vehicle. This is done by the instructors' positioning, and
communication with each other, the riders and other
road users.*

Before snaking you will need to decide the order of trainees in the line and agree with them some riding rules. The slowest riders, who may or may not be the least confident, ride towards the front of the snake and the stronger, faster and more confident riders towards the rear. The last trainee in the snake should be confident enough to be left at the back to signal to road users behind while the rear instructor moves forward occasionally (see below).

You will also have agreed these riding rules with your group:

- No overtaking
- Leave enough space to stop but not too much for a driver to cut into the snake (about a bike's length)
- Follow the line of the front instructor
- Remain silent and focussed (snakes are silent)

You are now set up to snake. Have a practice in the playground before going on the road to check your group are sticking to the rules and that you have put them in the correct order. If you notice a gap in the middle of the snake move the slow rider who causes the gap towards the front. Practise starting and stopping, encouraging riders to bunch up when they come to a stop.

Having an understanding of the different roles of each instructor will help you understand how to manage snaking.

Rear Instructor

- You are the first person on the road and the last to leave the road, In effect you are creating space in front of you to protect your trainees
- You anticipate the need for the snake to move right (or sometimes left) such as when changing lane on a multi lane road or to overtake a parked car. You move first so making space for the riders to move in front of you
- You arrive at Give Way situations (some junctions, roundabouts) before the group in order to ensure the group moves through without splitting up. You may need to request that a driver gives up their right of way occasionally
- You communicate to the front instructor when it's good to go through junctions or blind bends by being in the best position to observe this
- You arrive at locations where you may need to stop the snake or part of the snake (traffic lights, pedestrian crossings). You may need to take charge of the rear of the snake in these situations.
- You can observe and encourage riders in the snake who may be struggling by riding along side them and giving advice about their position or gear selection
- You inform the rear trainee that you are moving forward and ask them to check back and signal where necessary
- You manage drivers behind with positive communication using your body language and positioning to prevent inappropriate overtaking
- You thank drivers for their patience with a wave and a smile

Front instructor

- You are in charge, clearly communicating to trainees when to get on the road & when to start off
- You set the line in the road by your position which in most cases will be in primary position
- You pick locations to pull in where there is room for trainees to stop next to the kerb and leave the road
- You decide when to 'double up' making the snake shorter and wider, such as when approaching lights to get through quicker or when wishing to stop people overtaking when it may be risky
- You know the route and communicate any turns or lane changes early to the rear instructor to give them time to get into position
- You raise your hand high when signalling so the rear instructor can see your signal above the heads of the trainees
- You set the pace of the group by keeping the slowest rider behind you where you can monitor their speed

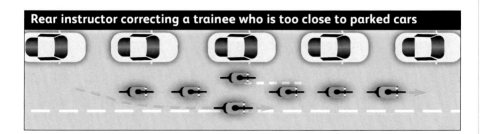

Rear instructor correcting a trainee who is too close to parked cars

The following diagrams illustrate how the two instructors work together in different situations:

Passing parked cars

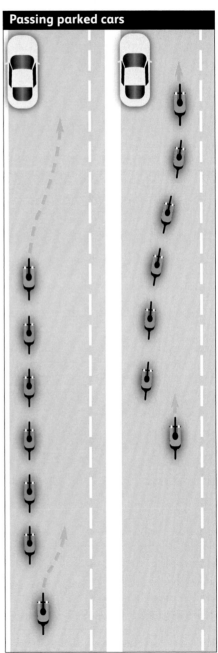

Left turn into major road

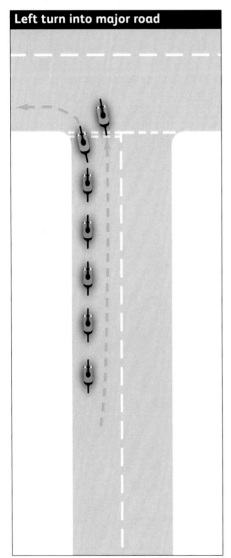

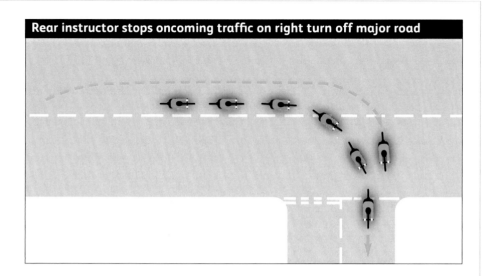

Rear instructor stops oncoming traffic on right turn off major road

8.2 Paired riding

This is a technique for moving a pair of trainees on road with only one instructor. This is useful for schools courses where time and funding allows for a reduction in the instructor:trainee ratio to 1:2 as well as family groups.

Before you go on road

Plan the locations and the route
• Plan with your co-instructor to ensure you each have appropriate locations
• Find a location close to the school for teaching the first activities
• Plan to limit right turns if possible, especially early on. Be prepared to cross roads on foot where that may be easier. They should be able to handle more complex turns once they have learnt some of the Level 2 syllabus
• Have a plan B

Family groups

Paired riding/ mini snaking is a useful technique for teaching families. Parents who wish to ride with their children would benefit from understanding some of the principals of paired riding. They may be surprised when they learn that they are better off positioned behind their children where they can protect them better and communicate with them more easily.

You do not have the right to direct traffic; however, it is common practice for teachers to halt the traffic when moving large groups of traffic across the road

Select your pair of riders. Consider these criteria:
- Social pairings – do the trainees want to train together?
- Skill level – you may wish to match the trainees who have similar skills, but sometimes a disparity in skills can work well and be beneficial to the weaker rider.
- Behavioural issues – you may not want to take a pair who don't get on or who both demonstrated problematic behaviour.
- Select the stronger rider to lead (initially).

Agree these ground rules specific to paired riding:
- Stay together close to the instructor where you can hear her.
- No overtaking.
- Second rider leaves enough room to stop between them and first rider, (about a bike's length).

Manage trainee's expectations
- Explain to your trainees how paired riding works and that you will be behind them and will be giving directions and encouragement from the back. (They will probably expect you to ride in front of them).
- Let them know where you plan to go, how long you'll be out and that they'll be stopping at various locations to learn.
- Tell them that you expect them to check behind to see where you are occasionally. This will develop their skills as well as enhance communication.

Practise the mini-snake in the playground
- Practise riding as a group in the playground before you go out on road. Ride in mini-snake formation in a straight line along the length of the playground, practise stopping. Pull up next to the front rider.
- Ask them to check behind and make eye contact with you.
- Give instructions to the front rider such as 'move to the right'. You can only go on road when you are sure the riders will follow your instructions.

Going on road

Teach the first and second riding activity (Level 2.1-2.6 & 2.7) close to the school

- They need to understand basic road positioning before you ride any distance with them.
- They must understand how junctions work and who goes first before they snake through a junction to ensure the front trainee stops and you always move through junctions together.
- Consider walking to the first location if conditions just outside the school are not ideal (e.g. no parked cars or it is too busy).

Use your positioning to protect them and communicate with them
- Ride to the right, next to the rear trainee initially.
- Be dynamic, move next to the front rider should you need to speak to them. They may not ride as you wish initially so keep giving them encouragement and guidance.
- Continually reinforce what you expect of them. As you move through the syllabus they should be putting what they learnt into practice, so will be riding a door's width from parked cars, checking down side road as they pass etc.
- Ensure they stop behind every Give Way line and wait for your cue before moving through junctions.
- Remember that they may not be clear about which is their right and left side. Check this before snaking and consider using other techniques such as your position and body language to indicate directions.
- Let both trainees have a go as the lead.
- Right turning major to minor is the most complex turn for paired riding. On the following page is a diagram showing how to do this:

Paired riding right turn major to minor

1. *Riders move to near centre of road*

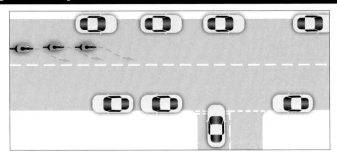

2. *Instructor overtakes trainees on left*

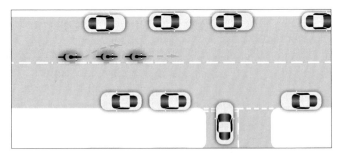

3. *Instructor moves ahead of trainees*

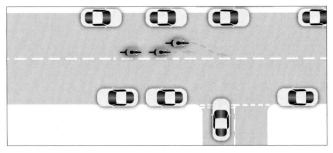

4. *Instructor moves ahead of trainees to stop oncoming traffic while group turns right off major road*

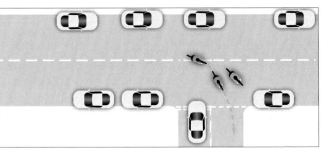

Running riding activities- general guidelines

Teach as usual with these additional considerations for teaching with1 instructor:
- You need to be able to see and be seen by both trainees at all times
- Lock bikes if you move away from them
- Consider running shorter riding activities both when you demonstrate and when trainees ride
- They should both be able to hear you at all times
- Each trainee should ride independently as usual so they get the 'outcome'
- Move around and be dynamic to ensure optimal visibility and communication with trainee and other road users

Running riding activities - specific guidelines

Beginning and ending a journey:
- Teach this outside the school. Consider a shorter run than usual. Position the non riding trainee half way along the routes so they can see. Move your position as they ride so they can always hear you

Passing side roads:
- Position yourself at the junction. Move towards where they end their journey so you can give feedback

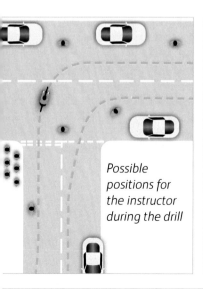

Possible positions for the instructor during the drill

Junction turns:

You may usually teach junctions turns combining 3 manoeuvres together (turning in and out of the major road and a U-turn). You will need to run each manoeuvre separately so you will be teaching 4 turns and a U-turn. (You could teach the U-turn when you teach beginning and ending a journey where you will be on a quieter road.) Teach 2 turns at one junction then move to a busier junction for the last pair of junction turns. Ensure the trainee who is not riding the activity can see so they can learn from their friend.

8.3 Moving individuals

When teaching an individual you can cover quite a distance riding with them. The environment you ride will depend on them and their aims. You may not be able to, nor need to, ride the route you will eventually use for an individual especially if they wish to take an advanced (Level 3) lesson or journey accompaniment exploring their route to work. It is good, however, that you have a general idea about the area you plan to use and the locations of key types of infrastructure such as traffic lights and roundabouts.

Ride behind your trainee to their right, especially when they begin to ride on road. Use this technique to move them to appropriate Level 2 locations. In this position you are shielding them from other road users ensuring that drivers pass them wide. You can also communicate with them and encourage them. You may however, be preventing them from observing what is behind and communicating with people. Move next to them at junctions and block for them as they move through junctions until they have learnt to do this themselves. Avoid filtering with your trainee at least until they reach Level 3 where filtering through traffic is part of the syllabus. If you move through a Level 3 environment (which is fine even for a trainee at Level 2 if managed well) stay in the traffic stream waiting your turn at lights.

When teaching them the riding activities consider riding the route of the activity with them (buddy riding) if they seem a little nervous. You must ensure that they ride each activity by themselves before progressing through the syllabus.

As they gain more confidence and progress through the syllabus, position yourself more directly behind them so you don't block their view and they are able to look back and communicate with other road users. You could even ride to their left to give them even more independence.

(Be sure to risk assess this for yourself as this position may put you close to parked cars).

There are occasions where you may decide to ride in front of your trainee either to demonstrate a technique such as filtering, enable them to communicate to people behind or to see if they can ride protectively of you so they have responsibility to shield you from drivers behind. This would be appropriate at a Level 3 session or when teaching a parent techniques for riding with their child.

By using your riding position dynamically with individuals, you can help build up a person's confidence quite quickly giving them more and more autonomy and control as the lesson progresses.

8.4 Walking with a group

It is always possible to walk with your group pushing their bikes. This can be a useful alternative to turning right across a busy road where there is a crossing. It may be useful when there is a traffic jam or to make a short trip to another teaching site nearby.

Here are some guidelines:

When walking along a pavement remain in single file so your group doesn't prevent people from walking past. Keep your group in a fixed (snake) order. Be courteous to people on foot stopping to let them pass. Thank anyone who you may inconvenience or who waits to let you and your group pass.

When crossing the road, ensure trainees cross between 2 instructors. Trainees line next to each other on the pavement, between 2 instructors, their front wheel facing the road they wish cross. When the road is clear everyone crosses together. Alternatively the instructors block both lanes (one blocking the nearside lane to the right and the offside lane to the left) and the trainee cross in a line between the instructors. In the latter instance the front instructor needs to get past the line and back into position at the front. Avoid crossing roads near junctions and blind turns unless an instructor is positioned where they can have a good line of sight to manage this.

8.5 Mass riding

Mass rides are a popular fun way of encouraging people, who may be wary of cycling, to ride on roads as part of a group protected from motorised traffic. The more people the better since mass rides can take up whole lanes or more and people taking part can socialise and party while marshals and ride leaders manage the ride and any risks. It is possible to run mass rides with a ratio of riders to marshals of around 8:1 increasing to 10:1 for more than 40 riders.

More detailed advice around running mass rides is outside the scope of this book. Many organisations (including Cycle Training UK) run ride leader/marshal training courses.

The principles for running mass rides are similar to snaking. The ride leader at the front must manage the speed and ensure people remain behind them. A rear marshal remains in a fixed position at the back. Other marshals ride ahead to block junctions and side roads preventing drivers from get stuck amongst the riders. Side riders ensure people in the mass don't stray into the oncoming traffic. Marshals rotate around the mass as shown in the diagram.

Risk of riders bumping into each other is higher than any conflict with other road users. This can be managed by encouraging the riders to leave a space between them and people in front. Controlling the speed is important. Encourage the slower riders, young people and family groups, to ride towards the front and ask faster riders to remain at the back to protect others. As long as everyone realises that the ride will be quite slow faster riders shouldn't get too frustrated.

Mass ride

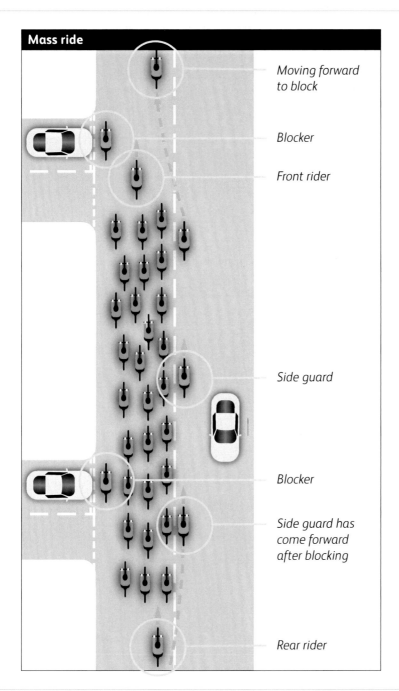

Moving forward
to block

Blocker

Front rider

Side guard

Blocker

Side guard has
come forward
after blocking

Rear rider

9.
Feedback and Monitoring

Knowing how and when to offer feedback and advice is crucial to keeping your trainee(s) on track and feeling positive. Here we will explore various points during and at the end of training when feedback is appropriate, and suggest ways of offering such advice that will benefit your trainee.

We will also look at the importance of evaluating and monitoring training outcomes for you, your scheme and for the whole cycle training sector.

9.1 Structuring feedback (the feedback sandwich)

The aim of feedback is to let trainees know how they are riding and what they need to do to improve

The aim of feedback is to let trainees know how they are riding and what they need to do to improve. It is also a tool to help trainees enjoy their training because of the continual positive reinforcement they receive from you. Feedback will also indicate to you that they are aware of their own ability and are able to asses their own riding. Whenever you offer some feedback during a session it is useful to elicit this self awareness from your trainee using this structure:

- What worked well
- What could have been better
- What will you do differently next time

Feedback can be elicited using statements and questions such as in this example:
Instructor: "That was a great emergency stop. What did you remember to do well?"
Jessica: "I used both brakes and braced my arms"
Instructor: "What about your feet?"
Jessica: "Oh yes, I put them on the ground too soon. Next time I'll stop the bike then put my feet down"

Sometimes rather than asking questions you could say the same thing in one sentence:
"Great emergency stop Jessica, you used both brakes and braced your arms though next time make sure the bike has stopped before you put your feet down"
This may be quicker when you are teaching a group and others are waiting to have a go.

9.2 Feedback during training

Trainees should know how they are doing throughout any session since you will be assessing their riding and giving them feedback all the time (See section 6.3). While you and your co-instructor will be giving a lot of feedback to each trainee as they ride, ask peers to observe and give feedback to each other as well. This will keep the young people engaged and they will learn from their friends' mistakes. You will need to teach them the feedback (sandwich) structure to ensure they keep things positive. Encouraging trainees to give feedback to each other will also ensure that they are observing each other and are more involved in the session. To give feedback, the trainees will need to be positioned where they can watch each other riding. This will also help towards ensuring good behaviour because they will not be hanging around in a big group waiting to ride.

There may be occasions when many trainees in your group make the same error. It is worth giving group feedback and even showing another demonstration when this happens. A general principle is to always input something between 'goes' so they improve rather than them repeating the same mistake again and again. While much training will be delivered to a group, riding outcomes are achieved as an individual riding alone so feedback should be specific to each person and where possible link to the trainees specific aims of learning to ride.

9.3 Feedback to individuals

When teaching individual adults it is worth discussing with them in detail their aims for the session and for the longer term, giving them an expectation of what they will achieve. You will be assessing them throughout the session as usual and in more detail at the end of a session where you should leave time to sit and discuss what they did well, what they need to practice and their next step (which may be booking another lesson with you). Refer to their aims to assess their progress. Ticking the boxes showing all the outcomes they have achieved can be very rewarding for them. Leave them with specific action points worded clearly with some indication of how to achieve these.

9.4 Ending a session

At the end of every session your trainees should feel positive and elated. There is little value in asking them to repeat a load of theory that they have already demonstrated so end the session on high. Some ways to bring a session to an end include asking them what was the most fun thing they did, or to suggest one point they'd tell their friend about riding a bike. Or simply tell them that they did brilliantly and let them go. If time allows, end with a short game in the playground. They should feel good and want to come back for more.

9.5 Ending a course

Depending on the funder or scheme, in addition to the feedback you may be required to issue badges and certificates or write reports for each trainee. Most Bikeability schemes have agreed to issue badges after all the compulsory outcomes have been achieved for each level. Some schemes issue certificates for people who took part even if they didn't finish the level. Such certificates should state that they are awarded for taking part and indicate for each trainee where they reached within the level and what they still need to complete for the badge.

It is important to be clear to the trainees and their parents what competencies they have achieved. If their trip to school is in a Level 2 environment and they have completed Level 2 - let them, their parents and the school know that they are able to ride to school. Suggest that perhaps they ride a couple of times with a parent first.

At the end of every session your trainees should feel positive and elated

9.6 Reflective practice

A good teacher is aware of how they performed, understanding that there is no such thing as a perfect session. Reflect on your own performance using the feedback structure and give yourself an action point for next time. Discuss each others performance with instructors that you have worked with and foster a culture of open feedback and constructive criticism within your organisation. This will ensure that you and your colleagues don't get complacent or stuck in a rut and are prepared to try new ways of teaching. This is great for professional development.

9.7 Feedback to your scheme and funders

It is a requirement of Bikeability and many commissioners of cycle training that they have records of who has been trained and what levels they reached. Many schemes would wish to know about any issues that arose during the session or any ideas that you may wish to share within your organisation. Questions to answer about any session or course could include the following:

- How many trainees attended?
- What level did they reach at the end of the session/course?
- How were the trainees learning/behaving?
- How were the logistics at the school?
- How was the support from your scheme?
- Any incidents? (If yes contact relevant people urgently and fill in appropriate documentation)
- How was the performance of instructors?
- What is the next step for cycling at the school?

Similar feedback is useful for individuals and other sessions such as maintenance.

9.8 Sector wide monitoring

There is great value in monitoring the effectiveness of training cyclists to the sector as a whole. In addition to monitoring the numbers trained and levels reached by trainees, finding out about the impact of training over a longer period will ensure continued funding and give a greater understanding of how a cycle training intervention could improve the nation's health and wellbeing, give young people more independence, improve people's driving skills, give other economic benefits and improve the places where we live work and study. Such surveys which will provide such data are currently being done and there is value to any scheme and instructor in contributing. The Association of Bikeability Schemes is engaged in gathering such data through its members and their links to schools.

9.9 Feedback to us

Cycle Training UK has evolved and developed since 1998 when the company requested feedback from every instructor and trainee who has been trained or worked for us. We would appreciate your thoughts about this book. Please get in touch letting us know what you liked about it, what you think would make the book better and any other thoughts. You will find our contact details at the front of the book,

Cycling makes
people healthier
and the spaces
where we live
more pleasant

Appendix 1: Safeguarding - Child Protection Awareness

This guidance was developed by child protection experts and has been agreed across all Bikeability schemes in England.

1.0 Introduction

These guidelines have been adapted from British Cycling's "Policy and Procedures for the protection of Children and Vulnerable Adults" (Jan 2007).

1.1 Entitlement

Everyone who participates in cycling activities is entitled to:
- An enjoyable and safe environment
- Care and protection from abuse

1.2 Obligations

Cycle Training organisations are obliged to devise and implement policies and procedures ensuring everyone involved in working with children is aware of their responsibility to:

- Safeguard children from harm and abuse
- Take action when necessary to safeguard children
- Report any concerns about the welfare of children in their care

1.3 Terms and Definitions

A **child** is anyone under the age of 18.
Working Together to Safeguard Children- DCFS 2010
www.education.gov.uk/publications/standard/ publicationdetail/page1/DCSF-00305-2010

A **vulnerable adult** is someone who is aged 18 years or over who 'is or may be in need of community care services by reason of mental health or other disability, age or illness' and 'is or may be unable to take care of him or herself, or unable to protect him or herself against significant harm or exploitation'. - No Secrets DOH 2000
www.dh.gov.uk/en/Publicationsandstatistics/ Publications/PublicationsPolicyAndGuidance/ DH_4008486

1.4 Acting on concerns

It is NOT the responsibility of Cycle Training organisations to determine whether or not abuse has taken place; this is the domain of child protection professionals (Social Services and the police), however the guidelines below will help identify what is meant by safe and unsafe practice.

Guidance on what to do if you are concerned about poor practice or possible abuse is given in section 4.

2.0 Good Practice

The Government issued guidance in 2009 for 'Safer Working Practice for adults who work with children and young people' – DCSF *webarchive.nationalarchives.gov. uk/20100202100434/dcsf.gov.uk/ everychildmatters/resources-and-practice/ig00311/*

Following the good practice guidelines listed below ensures that:
- all instructors operate within an agreed ethical framework
- cycling makes a positive contribution to the development of young people
- instructors are protected from false allegations of abuse or poor practice

2.1 Principles for safer working

All cycling instructors should adhere to the following principles:
- Ensure experience of cycling is fun and enjoyable; promote fairness, confront and deal with bullying and never condone byelaws / technical regulation violations or the use of prohibited substances
- Provide open access to all those who wish to participate in cycling and ensure they are treated fairly
- Ensure all cyclists are able to participate in an environment that is free from harassment, intimidation, victimisation, bullying and abuse.
- Be an excellent role model, do not drink alcohol or smoke when working with young people
- Treat all young people and vulnerable adults equally; this means giving both the more and less talented in a group similar attention, time, respect and dignity.
- Respect the developmental stage of each young person. This means ensuring that the training intensity is appropriate to the physical, social and emotional developmental stage of the cyclist. Ensure training and riding schedules are based on the needs and interests of the child, not those of the parents, organisers, coaches, trainee coaches and leaders or clubs
- Conduct all coaching and meetings in an open environment; avoid one-to-one coaching in unobserved situations

- Maintain a safe and appropriate relationship with cyclists; it is inappropriate to have an intimate relationship with a young person. (It is a criminal offence for someone in a position of trust to have a sexual relationship with 16-17 year olds in their care- Sexual Offences Act 2003)
- Build relationships based on mutual trust and respect in which young people are encouraged to take responsibility for their own development and decision-making
- Avoid unnecessary physical contact with young people. Touching can be okay and appropriate as long as it is neither intrusive nor disturbing. Always ensure the cyclist's permission has been given
- Where supervision is required, involve parent volunteers, guardians or carer's, wherever possible and ensure that adults work in pairs
- Communicate regularly with parents, involve them in decision-making and gain written consent for all training. Secure their consent in writing to act in loco parentis, if the need arises to give permission for the administration of emergency first aid and/or other medical treatment
- Be aware of any medical conditions (including allergies), existing injuries and medicines being taken. Keep a written record of any injury or accident that occurs, together with details of any treatment given. Ensure you are qualified and up-to-date in first aid or that there is someone with a first aid qualification in attendance
- Keep up to date with the technical skills, qualifications and insurance in cycling
- All instructors, members, volunteers and employees will be expected to abide by a 'Code of Conduct' as outlined by their Bikeability scheme

3.0 Poor or Unsafe Practice

Being aware of what is considered poor practice may help protect instructors from false allegations and give indications of possible abuse

3.1 Examples of unsafe activity

Instructors should avoid the following examples of poor practice:
- Spending a lot of time with one child away from the others
- Taking children into instructor's home or entering into the child's home alone
- Engaging in rough, physical or sexually provocative play
- Engaging in any form of inappropriate touching
- Allowing children to use inappropriate language (without challenging them)
- Making sexually suggestive comments to a child, even in fun
- Making a child cry (as a form of control)
- Allowing allegations made by a child to go unchallenged unrecorded or not acted upon
- Doing things of a personal nature for children or vulnerable adults that they can do for themselve
- Tolerating bullying, rule violations or use of prohibited substances
- Showing favouritism towards one cyclist or the giving or receiving of gifts
- Wearing clothing that is distracting, revealing or sexually provocative
- Encourage or allow social contact outside of the training session either by phone, Email or social networks.
- Take images of cyclists for personal use
- Behave in a manner which may compromise their suitability to work with vulnerable groups. i.e. criminal activities

3.2 Keeping people informed

If cases arise where situations mentioned above are unavoidable they should only occur with the full knowledge of the leader of the session, the Cycle Training organisation and the child's parents.

The above people should also be informed if any of the following incidents should occur:
- If an instructor accidentally hurts a child cyclist
- If a child seems distressed in any manner
- If a child appears to be sexually aroused by an instructor's actions
- If a child misunderstands or misinterprets something an instructor has done

4.0 Responding to disclosure, suspicion or allegations

While it is not the responsibility of instructors to identify abuse, it is their responsibility to report any concerns about the welfare of a child or vulnerable adult. Such concerns may arise because:
- A young person or vulnerable adult discloses s/he is being abused
- Of the behaviour of an adult towards a child
- Of observation of examples of poor practice (see above)
- Of observation of indicators of abuse and bullying (See appendix)

4.1 Reporting procedures

All organisations endorsing these guidelines should have an employee to act as the designated Safeguarding Lead. (S.L.).

Organisations should also be aware of their Local Safeguarding Children's and Adults Boards L.S.C.B. and L.S.A.B's Policy and Procedures.

Any person with information of a disclosure, allegation or suspicion about the welfare of a child or vulnerable adult must immediately report this in one of the following ways.

- Inform your Safeguarding Lead (S.L.)
- If you are working in a school inform the head teacher who will follow the normal LSCB and Local Authority Designated Officer procedures (LADO)
- In cases where the S.L. is unavailable you should take responsibility and seek advice from the duty officer at a local social services department Safeguarding Unit/Team or your local police. You must then also inform your S.L. as soon as possible

4.2 Dealing with complaints against an employee

Where there is a complaint against a Cycling Instructor there may be three types of investigation.

- Criminal: in which case the police are immediately involved
- Safeguarding Complaint: Complaint directed to the Safeguarding Lead (S.L.) for referral to social services and possibly the police will be involved
- Disciplinary or misconduct: in which case the Training organisation will be involved

While the S.L. and child welfare officers will have received training they are not experts, it is not their responsibility to determine whether abuse has taken place. If there is any doubt about whether or not the alleged behaviour constitutes abuse, the concern must be shared with professional agencies

4.3 Dealing with Safeguarding Allegations

Any suspicion that a child has been abused by either an employee or a volunteer should be reported immediately to the S.L. who will take appropriate steps to ensure the safety of the child or vulnerable in question and any other child who may be at risk. This will include the following:

- Refer the allegation to the social care services safeguarding unit/team who may involve the police or
- In an emergency go directly to the police
- Contact the parents of the child/ adult as soon as possible following advice from the social care services department

The Chief Executive or Director of your Bikeability scheme should be notified who will decide on media enquiries and disciplinary action. Considerations will be given towards imposing an interim suspension based on the risk to the child, the serious nature of the allegation and the need to ensure a full investigation can be instituted.

4.4 Historic Allegations

Allegations of abuse may be made some time after the event (e.g. by an adult who was abused as a child or by a member of staff who is still currently working with children). Where such an allegation is made, your Bikeability scheme will follow the same procedures and report the matter to the social care services or the police. This is because other children, either within or outside cycling, may be at risk from this person. Anyone who has a previous criminal conviction for offences related to abuse is automatically excluded from working with children

4.5 Recording Concerns

You should make a detailed record at the time of the disclosure/concern (your organisation should have a form to use). Information should be written in factual format, avoiding any opinion or hearsay and should include the following:

- The facts about the allegation or observation
- A description of any visible bruising, other injuries or signs
- The child or adult's account, if this has been disclosed, of what has happened and how any bruising or other injuries occurred
- Any witnesses to the incident(s).
- Any times, dates or other relevant information
- A clear distinction between what is fact, opinion or hearsay
- A copy of this information should be sent to the S.L.

Reporting the matter to the police or social care services department should not be delayed by attempts to obtain more information. Wherever possible, referrals telephoned to the social care services department should be confirmed in writing within 24 hours. A record should also be made of the name and designation of the social care services member of staff or police officer to whom the concerns were passed, together with the time and date of the call, in case any follow-up is needed.

4.6 Storage of Confidential

Safeguarding information
Safeguarding information should be stored in a secure location in line with data protection laws with access available only to authorised personnel.

Appendix 2: Supplementary Materials

Cycle Training UK's team of instructors have published additional training guides that you may find useful to enhance your work as a cycle trainer.

Teaching New Cyclists
A guide for training someone who has never ridden.

Cycling Games Compendium.
Games to enhance the fun of learning to ride.

These can be ordered from Cycle Training UK's online shop: www.cycletraininguk.com

Other useful resources can be found on Cycle Training UK's resource section including classroom lessons for teachers, surveys about the effectiveness of training and other papers as well as a series of case studies showing the extent of work possible for a cycle trainer.